# HOLT

# A World History Teacher's Guide to Analyzing Movies

**HOLT, RINEHART AND WINSTON**

A Harcourt Education Company

Orlando • Austin • New York • San Diego • London

**For permission to reproduce copyrighted material, grateful acknowledgment is made to the following sources:**

From "The Confrontation with a Murderer" by Thomas T. Blatt from *Sobibor – The Forgotten Revolt* web site, accessed November 14, 2006, at http://www.sobibor.info/confrontation.html. Copyright © 1984 by **Thomas T. Blatt.** Reproduced by permission of the author. From *Liberal Religion, Part II* by Davidson Loehr. Copyright © 2005 by **Davidson Loehr.** Reproduced by permission of the author. From an unpublished email by Davidson Loehr. Copyright © 2006 by **Davidson Loehr.** Reproduced by permission of the author. From *The Samurai: A Military History* by S. R. Turnbull. Copyright © 1977 by S. R. Turnbull. Reproduced by permission of **Macmillan Publishing Co., Inc.** From *A History of Russia,* Fourth Edition by Nicholas V. Riasanovsky. Copyright © 1963, 1969, 1977, 1984 by **Oxford University Press, Inc.** Reproduced by permission of the publisher. From "A Suffolk Farmhand at Gallipoli, June 1915" by Leonard Thompson from *Akenfield* by Ronald Blythe. Copyright © 1969 by Ronald Blythe. Reproduced by permission of **Pantheon Books, a division of Random House, Inc., www.randomhouse.com.** From "An African View of European Expansion" from *Facing Mount Kenya* by Jomo Kenyatta. Copyright 1953 by Jomo Kenyatta. Reproduced by permission of **Seeker and Warburg.** From "With Austrian Cavalry on the Eastern Front, August 1915" from *My Life* by Oskar Kokoschka, translated by David Britt. Copyright © 1974 by David Britt. Reproduced by permission of **Thames and Hudson.** From *The Rule Statutes of the Teutonic Knights,* translated by Indrikis Sterns. Copyright © 1969 by Indrikis Sterns. Reproduced by permission of **University Press of America, a division of Rowman Publishers.** From "En-Hedu-Ana's Lawsuit in the poem Nin-me-sara" by En-Hedu-Ana from *Der Rechtsfall der Enheduanna im Lied Nin-me-sarra,* translated by Annette Zgoll. Copyright © 1997 by **Annette Zgoll.** Reproduced by permission of the author.

ISBN-13 978-0-0-3093820-7

ISBN 0-03-093820-1

2 3 4 5 6 7 8 9  912 12 11 10 09 08 07

# Contents

## A World History Teacher's Guide to Analyzing Movies

To the Teacher .................................................................................................................... iv

**Intolerance**
Ancient Mesopotamia ....................................................................................................... 1

**The Odyssey**
Greek Mythology ............................................................................................................... 5

**Ben-Hur**
Rome ................................................................................................................................... 9

**Alexander Nevsky**
Early Russia ....................................................................................................................... 13

**Becket**
The Middle Ages ............................................................................................................... 17

**Shogun**
Early Japan ......................................................................................................................... 21

**The Mission**
Exploration and Colonization ......................................................................................... 25

**A Man For All Seasons**
The Reformation in England ............................................................................................ 29

**The Leopard**
Italian Unification ............................................................................................................. 33

**Zulu**
Imperialism in Africa ....................................................................................................... 37

**All Quiet on the Western Front**
World War I ........................................................................................................................ 41

**Dr. Zhivago**
The Russian Revolution .................................................................................................... 45

**Escape from Sobibor**
The Holocaust .................................................................................................................... 49

**The Jewel in the Crown**
Indian Independence ......................................................................................................... 53

**Thirteen Days**
The Cold War ..................................................................................................................... 57

Teacher's Guide to Analyzing Movies

## Using Movies in the Classroom

Movies can provide information and reinforce concepts in a way that interests and motivates students like no other teaching tool. In addition, movies vividly convey the drama of past events and the details of daily life in other places and times. The characters engage students' interest from an emotional perspective.

Movies are also useful as historical documents, and can be "read" like any other. By teaching students how to read a film in terms of visual language, bias, and intended purpose, teachers can help students develop the critical viewing skills necessary in today's visually oriented society. Using movies in a history classroom allows students to practice their media literacy skills while providing historical content in an interesting way.

Feature films, however, are neither recordings of actual events nor documentaries. Instead, movies are interpretations made with particular goals. The questions a film raises and the viewpoints it presents are drawn as much from the time period in which the film was made as from the time period of the events shown on the screen. This means that using film in the classroom can be a complex undertaking. In order to judge a film's viewpoint, students have to understand not just the events covered by a film, but also the era in which the film was created.

## Using This Guide

The movie scenes in this guide were chosen because they are useful in helping students discuss historical content as well as interpretations of that content. Although the selected scenes are appropriate for most middle school and high school students, personal and community standards vary. Before using a movie activity, you are strongly encouraged to preview the specific scenes. If possible, view the entire film. Please note that some scenes in the films may not be appropriate for your students, so take special care if you decide to use scenes that are not highlighted in this guide. Time measurements are given for the DVD version of the film. Previewing to adjust for differences in time measurement among video and DVD players is also recommended.

## Using the Activities

There is a set of four pages for each film. You may use the pages however you wish; using them all should fill a typical class period. Here is one possible lesson plan that uses all four pages:

**Prepare** Read "Why Watch This Movie?" on the first Movie Guide page aloud to the class. Help students understand the historical context of the film's events, as well as the context of the times in which the movie was made.

**Teach** Read "The Scenes" aloud and show the highlighted scenes to the class. You may duplicate the Guided Viewing Activity page for students to complete while watching the scenes.

**Assess** Use the discussion questions to explore students' reactions and to ensure that they understand the scenes. The paragraphs titled "What can students learn from these scenes?" can help you focus class discussion. If you wish, pause after each scene and discuss it before continuing to the next one. Or, you may want to have students write down their responses. Use "What happens next? How does the story end?" for the full context of the story and its times. Note that there are additional discussion questions if you choose to show the entire film.

**Extend** Use the Reading Like a Historian page to connect the film more closely to historical events. Discussion questions for these pages help students make comparisons between written sources and what they see on the screen. You may duplicate these pages so students can read the passages for themselves. Simply cover the answers at the bottom of the page before you photocopy it.

> 1916; D. W. Griffith, Director; Starring Mae Marsh, Robert Harron, Lillian Gish, Miriam Cooper, Constance Talmadge, Eugene Pallette, and Erich von Stroheim
> 177 minutes, not rated, available on videotape and DVD, black and white

## WHY WATCH THIS MOVIE?

*Intolerance* provides a glimpse into life in Mesopotamia in 539 BC, as the Babylonian Empire is about to fall to Persian invaders. The High Priest of Bel is angry that Prince Belshazzar has permitted the worship of the god Ishtar. In order to defend his beliefs and his position, the High Priest betrays his people.

The film's director, D. W. Griffith, is regarded as one of the great motion picture directors of the 1900s. He is best known for *The Birth of a Nation* (1915), a portrayal of the American Reconstruction era that remains controversial. Griffith thought that *Intolerance* was his masterpiece. However, the movie received mixed reviews from critics and failed at the box office. Griffith took years to repay the debts he incurred while making it.

*Intolerance* was expensive to make because it was an ambitious project. Griffith weaves together four stories from different historical periods: the modern era, Judea during the life of Jesus, the massacre of French Protestants in 1572, and ancient Babylon. The film cuts back and forth between the various stories to illustrate the negative consequences of religious and social intolerance. The Babylon story fits into the film's theme. According to the film, had the High Priest accepted religious tolerance, catastrophe would not have befallen the Babylonians.

## THE SCENES

**Scene 1** (from 00:04:00 to 00:26:15, 22 minutes) opens outside Babylon's gates, showing the hustle and bustle of a dynamic, cosmopolitan trading city. Major characters, including the fictional Mountain Girl and the historic Prince Belshazzar, are introduced. The religious conflict between Belshazzar and the priests of Bel-Marduk is reflected in the anger of the High Priest at the celebration of the rival goddess, Ishtar. The power of Babylon is reflected in the opening of the massive city gates. The scene concludes with the court sending Mountain Girl to find a husband.

**Scene 2** (from 01:14:45 to 01:19:30, 5 minutes) begins with the High Priest of Bel furious at the worship of Ishtar. Meanwhile, the Persian forces prepare to attack Babylon. A priest of Bel-Marduk supplies information to help Cyrus conquer the city.

**Scene 3** (from 01:29:50 to 01:47:30, 17 minutes) starts with the Persians laying siege to the city walls. Mountain Girl disguises herself and takes up arms against the enemy. An epic battle ensues, with the Persians using engines of war to break the Babylonian defense. The people of the city make sacrifices and offers prayers to Ishtar. All seems lost, but the Babylonians repulse the Persian attack.

## DISCUSSION QUESTIONS BASED ON THE SCENES

1. How is Babylon depicted in Griffith's film? What sources of conflict in Babylonian society are shown? *Possible answers: Students might note that Griffith offers a positive portrayal of Babylon. The city is large, well defended, and filled with statues and magnificent architecture. The Babylonians have a working court system. The citizens, like Mountain Girl, are brave, and Belshazzar is a tolerant ruler. The only conflict depicted in the film is the traitorous behavior of the priests of Bel.*

Teacher's Guide to Analyzing Movies

2. How is Cyrus the Great portrayed? What do the battle scenes reveal about war in ancient Babylon? *Possible answers: Cyrus is portrayed as a cruel conqueror, the opposite of his counterpart, Prince Belshazzar. Battle is depicted as chaotic and deadly and filled with various weapons of war needed to destroy the city walls.*

## WHAT CAN STUDENTS LEARN FROM THESE SCENES?

Students learn about some aspects of Babylonian culture. To make *Intolerance* as historically accurate as possible at that time, Griffith created a research department. He read recent scholarship on Babylonian history and used information obtained from archaeological digs to build the enormous sets. Thus, students can gain some idea of the grandeur of Babylon.

To stage the battle sequences, Griffith used sources such as the works of the Greek historian Herodotus. As shown in the film, warriors at this time used siege towers to attack city walls. Catapults and burning oil were standard weapons of the day. However, the director did engage in some creative thinking. Elephants were not used to push siege towers, and no records describe a giant flamethrower in any battles at this time.

Griffith deviates from the historical record for dramatic purposes. Historians are not certain that the priests of Bel-Marduk were traitors, although some scholars have argued that they betrayed the city. Scholars regard Griffith's portrayal of Cyrus as unfair. Nonetheless, the film earns high marks for Griffith's efforts to re-create ancient Babylon.

## WHAT HAPPENS NEXT? HOW DOES THE STORY END?

The Babylonians hold a celebration. Meanwhile, the priests of Bel conspire to aid the Persians. Mountain Girl learns of the plot, but she does not convince Belshazzar until it is too late. The priests let the Persians in through the city gates. The city is lost, and Belshazzar commits suicide. Mortally wounded by a Persian arrow, Mountain Girl witnesses the devastation as she dies.

## IF YOUR CLASS WATCHES THE ENTIRE FILM

The myths of Greece and the might of the Roman Empire have long attracted filmmakers. However, they have largely ignored other empires of the ancient world. Griffith sought to draw attention to the Babylonians and portrayed their achievements in a positive light. Why have directors neglected the histories of other ancient societies? Which civilization that you have studied in previous classes do you believe would be a good subject for a historical film? Explain your choice. *Possible answers: Moviegoers are much more familiar with the histories of Greece and Rome. Film producers may be worried that making a film about a different society would fail to attract a large audience. Students will select different ancient societies about which to make a film. Have them discuss their reasons in class.*

## GUIDED VIEWING ACTIVITY ANSWERS

1. He sees the new religion as a threat to his own power.

2. Mountain Girl must go to the marriage market and find a husband.

3. The Persian forces include Medes, Ethiopians, and barbarians.

4. She disguises herself as a soldier and joins the battle.

5. Weapons used include swords, spears, bows, siege towers, catapults, and burning oil.

*Intolerance*

# Guided Viewing Activity

## Ancient Mesopotamia

## SCENE 1

1. How does the High Priest react to the arrival of Ishtar?

_____

_____

_____

2. What does the court order Mountain Girl to do?

_____

_____

_____

## SCENE 2

3. What forces have gathered to aid the Persians?

_____

_____

_____

## SCENE 3

4. What does Mountain Girl do during the Persian attack?

_____

_____

_____

5. What weapons are used during the battle?

_____

_____

_____

## Analyzing Primary Sources

These documents from before and after the Persian conquest of Babylon may enhance your viewing of *Intolerance*.

**Source 1: From a hymn to Inanna (Ishtar) by a Sumerian priestess**

"That you annihilate rebelling territories, shall be known!
That you roar against the enemy lands, shall be known!
That you crush the leaders, shall be known!
That you devour corpses like a predator, shall be known!
That your glance is terrible, shall be known!
That you raise your terrible glance, shall be known!"

—Enheduanna, "The Exaltation of Inanna," c. 2285–2250 BC

**For Discussion** Enheduanna, who was the daughter of Sargon the Great, is the first author known by name. Her hymn praises Inanna, also called Ishtar, the Mesopotamian goddess whose worship causes conflict in *Intolerance.* Ishtar was a goddess of both love and war. Why might people of an early civilization combine love and war in the same goddess?

**Source 2: From Herodotus, on the city of Babylon**

"Assyria possesses a vast number of great cities, whereof the most renowned and strongest at this time was Babylon, where, after the fall of Nineveh, the seat of government had been removed . . . While such is its size, in magnificence there is no other city that approaches to it . . . In the time of Cyrus there was likewise in this temple a figure of a man, twelve cubits [about 18 feet] high, entirely of solid gold. I myself did not see this figure, but I relate what the Chaldaeans report."

—Herodotus, from *The History of the Persian Wars*, c. 430 BC

**For Discussion** How does the description by Herodotus compare to the film's depiction of the city? In this passage, how does Herodotus show that he tried to be a responsible historian?

## ANSWERS

**Source 1** *Possible answer: Both love and war are strong emotions, and both are part of the cycle of birth and death—a cycle that people of an early civilization would have known well.*

**Source 2** *Possible answers: The written description echoes the magnificence shown in the film. Herodotus reports what he had been told, but is honest about not having seen the statue himself.*

1997; Andrei Konchalovsky, Director; Starring Armand Assante, Greta Scacchi, Isabella Rossellini, Vanessa Williams, Bernadette Peters, and Eric Roberts

165 minutes, rated PG-13, available on videotape and DVD, color

This activity applies to the 1997 television miniseries. There is also a 1992 film with the same name.

## WHY WATCH THIS MOVIE?

*The Odyssey* is a condensed retelling of Homer's epic poem of the same name. Along with Homer's other epic poem, the *Iliad,* which recounts events of the Trojan War itself, the *Odyssey* is a classic of world literature. The two poems tell not just of the battle between the Greeks and the Trojans, but also of the wanderings of the cursed Odysseus, one of the Greek warriors. Like the epic poem, the film is filled with titanic battles, vengeful gods, and horrific monsters.

The miniseries begins with a condensed version of the Trojan War, including the story of the Trojan horse. (The episode is mentioned in the *Odyssey,* but the most detailed version of the Trojan horse story appears in the *Aeneid,* by Virgil, a Roman poet.) The remainder of the series is based more closely on Homer's *Odyssey* and includes several well-known scenes such as the battle with the Cyclops and the bewitching enchantments of the sorceress Circe. These tales are the source of many people's understanding of Greek myths and have introduced countless generations to the Greek gods and goddesses.

Filmmakers have long been drawn to Homer's works and to Greek mythology in general. The first film featuring the adventures of Odysseus was released in 1905. There have been at least 16 movies based on the *Iliad* and the *Odyssey*. The 1997 television miniseries received an Emmy award for outstanding directing.

## THE SCENES

**Scene 1** (from 00:12:56 to 00:25:14, 12 minutes) opens as Odysseus, King of Ithaca, has reluctantly left his wife Penelope and their newborn son Telemachus to join his fellow Greeks in battle against Troy. Achilles kills the great Trojan warrior Hector and drags his body behind a chariot. Odysseus' mother awaits the return of her son, but the war drags on as Achilles dies in battle. Demoralized, the Greeks consider surrender, but Odysseus concocts a scheme to defeat Troy. His men build a great wooden horse that the Trojans believe is a gift left behind by the fleeing Greeks. The Trojans drag the horse into their city, unaware that Greek soldiers are hidden inside. Once within the city gates, Odysseus and his men climb out of the horse and fight the Trojans. Intoxicated with victory, Odysseus brags to the gods. Poseidon, god of the sea, punishes Odysseus for not acknowledging the aid the Greeks have received from him and other gods. He tells Odysseus that he will never see his homeland of Ithaca again.

**Scene 2** (from 01:18:3 to 01:28:33, 10 minutes) starts with Odysseus and his crew, who have been lost for five years. In order to find the route to Ithaca, Odysseus journeys to Hades, the underworld. The prophet Tiresias tells the lost Greek how to return to his home. As he leaves the underworld, Odysseus meets his mother, who has killed herself out of grief for her missing son.

**Scene 3** (from 01:33:11 to 01:39:00, 6 minutes) opens with the Greeks passing through a narrow strait. Scylla, a three-headed beast, kills several crew members. After evading Scylla, Odysseus and his men are drawn into Charybdis, a monster that resembles a whirlpool. The ship is destroyed, but Odysseus survives.

## DISCUSSION QUESTIONS BASED ON THE SCENES

1. How do the Greeks use supernatural or monstrous beings to explain the natural world in these scenes? *Possible answer: The Greeks attribute many natural events to supernatural beings. For example, Poseidon controls the waves in the sea. In addition, the Greeks explain natural events such as the whirlpool as the behavior of the monster Charybdis.*

2. What conclusions can you draw regarding Greek religious beliefs from these scenes? *Possible answer: The Greeks were polytheists, or believers in many gods. The Greek gods are often cruel and act on petty emotions such as jealousy or pride. The Hades scene indicates that, for the Greeks, the afterlife was a place of pain and punishment that mortals could visit—at least under extraordinary circumstances.*

## WHAT CAN STUDENTS LEARN FROM THESE SCENES?

Students learn about the role of the gods in the lives of ancient Greeks. The miniseries shows that the gods felt many human emotions including pride, anger, and desire. Students also learn about Homer's epic poems. However, the movie omits several of Odysseus's adventures, especially one of the most famous, his conflict with the Sirens. The film's depiction of Hades can provide insight into Greek conceptions of the afterlife.

## WHAT HAPPENS NEXT? HOW DOES THE STORY END?

The shipwrecked Odysseus escapes the clutches of the nymph Calypso, who wants him to remain on her island. At sea on a small raft, Odysseus again meets with Poseidon, who tells the suffering Greek that, without the gods, man is nothing. Later, a friendly king returns the long-lost sailor to Ithaca, where Odysseus learns that his family faces threats. Suitors who seek to marry Penelope plot to kill Telemachus, who is convinced his father is still alive. Athena disguises Odysseus as an old man. The returning king kills the suitors, the disguise is lifted, and Odysseus is reunited with his family. *Note: Some scenes are sexually suggestive.*

## IF YOUR CLASS WATCHES THE ENTIRE FILM

Greek mythology has long attracted filmmakers, but Greek history has received little attention from the motion picture industry. Why do filmmakers prefer myths to history? If you were to make a movie about Greek history, what event or person would you use as your subject? *Possible answers: Many people are familiar with Greek myths, while few know details regarding Greece's history. More important, the Greek myths offer directors the opportunity to load their films with special effects, which will draw audiences to theaters. Students will select different historical events or personages when discussing their plans for a movie based on Greek history.*

## GUIDED VIEWING ACTIVITY ANSWERS

1. He hits him with a spear and then drags him behind a chariot.

2. Laocoön is killed by a sea serpent sent by Poseidon.

3. The soothsayer tells Odysseus to follow the constellation Orion.

4. He meets his mother, who has committed suicide.

5. Scylla is a many-headed beast that bites the Greeks. Charybdis is an enormous whirlpool with teeth that pulls the Greeks to their deaths by drowning.

Name _____ Class _____ Date _____

**The Odyssey**

**SCENE 1**

1. How does Achilles defeat Hector?

_____

_____

_____

2. What happens to Laocoön, the soothsayer who warns the Trojans against accepting the wooden horse?

_____

_____

_____

_____

**SCENE 2**

3. What route does Tiresias tell Odysseus to follow?

_____

_____

_____

4. Whom does Odysseus meet as he leaves Hades?

_____

_____

_____

**SCENE 3**

5. What do Scylla and Charybdis look like? How do they kill the Greeks?

_____

_____

_____

## Analyzing Primary Sources

These quotations may enhance your viewing of *The Odyssey*:

### From a scholar of theology

"The Greeks had both teachings and stories. But their gods were intended from the start as symbols of, projections of, the natural forces around and within us. Gods like Zeus and Poseidon were responsible for thunderstorms or storms at sea, as Demeter controlled the growing of the crops and Hestia gave us the subtle ability to add human feeling to worship and home . . .

Other gods and goddesses were personifications of some of the psychological styles that have always been part of human nature. The war-making, angry spirit familiar to many men came from Ares, the god of war. Our cleverness, as well as our ability to understand subtle and sacred meanings in things came from Hermes. Women whose lives revolved around the care of their children were the daughters of Demeter, as those with a fierce and focused ambition claimed Artemis . . .

So these gods and goddesses weren't really about supernatural creatures, but about the dimensions of our world and of ourselves that always set the stage for our lives, and that seem to drive us through them. The Olympic Greek gods and goddesses—originally they had six male and six female deities—were aspects of the human experience writ large, rather than distant and unrelated powers we must appease. When Muslims say that Allah is closer to them than their own jugular vein, they are showing the kind of awareness from within which the Greek gods were created and clothed."

—Davidson Loehr, Ph.D., *Liberal Religion, Part II,* 2005

"The Greek gods were personifications of enduring/eternal natural and psychological dynamics—not necessarily *good* ones, just *powerful* ones."

—Davidson Loehr, Ph.D., unpublished e-mail, 2006

**For Discussion** These passages focus on the Greek gods' personification of human qualities. Do Poseidon and Odysseus share any qualities? If so, which? Of Poseidon and Odysseus, which one appears to be more noble? On what do you base your opinion?

## ANSWERS

*Possible answers: Poseidon and Odysseus are both violent and capable of great rage. Odysseus eventually appears to be more noble than Poseidon. Students should support their statements.*

1959; William Wyler, Director; Starring Charlton Heston, Jack Hawkins, Haya Harareet, Stephen Boyd, Hugh Griffith, Martha Scott, and Cathy O'Donnell

212 minutes, not rated, available on videotape and DVD, color

This activity applies to the 1959 original of the film. Other versions were produced in 1907 and 1925. Animated versions were released in 1980 and 2002.

## WHY WATCH THIS MOVIE?

*Ben-Hur* remains one of the most powerful epic films ever produced. It brilliantly captures the might and brutality of ancient Rome. Its hero, Judah Ben-Hur, is a Jewish aristocrat in first-century Judea. His childhood friend Messala, now a Roman tribune, seeks assistance in suppressing a Jewish rebellion against Roman rule. Judah refuses. Messala finds an opportunity to sentence him to service as a galley slave. Enraged at this betrayal, Judah vows revenge. In the years that follow he will meet Jesus, spend three years as a galley slave, take part in a major naval battle, and became the greatest charioteer in Rome.

    The 1959 epic was the third motion picture based on the 1880 novel by Lew Wallace. To capture the grandeur of Rome, the movie's producers spent $15 million, making *Ben-Hur* the most expensive motion picture made up to that time. Their investment paid off—the film won 11 Academy Awards and remained one of the top moneymaking films through the mid-1970s. The chariot race, which took three months to produce, is still considered one of the finest action sequences ever filmed.

## THE SCENES

**Scene 1** (from 01:17:18 to 01:26:13, 9 minutes) depicts a naval battle between Romans and pirates. Judah, a galley slave for three years, has impressed Roman tribune Quintus Arrius. During the battle the ship is rammed, and Judah saves Arrius's life.

**Scene 2** (from 02:42:44 to 02:53:44, 11 minutes) portrays the culmination of Judah's conflict with Messala. Freed from bondage and adopted by Arrius, Judah has returned to Judea. Told that his mother and sister died in prison, he seeks his revenge against Messala in a chariot race. The two men battle one another while speeding around the arena. Messala is mortally injured in a chariot accident.

## DISCUSSION QUESTIONS BASED ON THE SCENES

1. What do scenes 1 and 2 indicate about Roman attitudes toward human life? *Possible answer: Students might note that these scenes reveal callousness toward human life. The galley slaves are beaten if they do not perform adequately and are left to die when the ship sinks. At the chariot races, the crowds cheer when the drivers are injured or killed and show little emotion over the fate of Messala.*

2. Why do you think the Romans held events such as chariot races? *Possible answer: In addition to providing entertainment for the masses, large-scale events such as chariot races reflected the power of Rome and awed spectators.*

## WHAT CAN STUDENTS LEARN FROM THESE SCENES?

Students learn from the galley sequence the tremendous manpower necessary to sustain Rome's military might. (Rome, however, did not use slaves to man galleys during the first century.) The chariot race is accurate in many ways. Spectacles such as these attracted huge audiences and served to bring together people of different backgrounds, much as modern professional sports do today. The Circus Maximus, the largest venue, could seat nearly 250,000 spectators. Teams of two or four horses pulled the chariot around a circular track. As shown in the film, races began when a consul dropped a white handkerchief. Charioteers completed seven laps on a track nearly a mile long, for a total of six miles per race. Metal dolphin markers were used to keep track of laps. However, the typical race consisted of only four chariots, rather than the nine shown at the start of the contest in *Ben-Hur*.

## WHAT HAPPENS NEXT? HOW DOES THE STORY END?

The dying Messala tells Judah that his mother and sister are alive but have been infected with leprosy, a disfiguring disease that made outcasts of its victims. Judah angrily refuses to accept citizenship in the Roman Empire, declaring that Rome destroyed his friend Messala and his family. He rejects love in favor of revenge. However, the servant girl Esther convinces him to take his mother and sister to meet a rabbi preaching a message of salvation. Judah has the opportunity to aid Jesus on the way to his death by crucifixion. Upon Jesus' death, the two women are cured of leprosy, and Judah feels the anger lifted from his heart.

## IF YOUR CLASS WATCHES THE ENTIRE FILM

The Roman Empire has long fascinated filmmakers. However, many motion pictures, ranging from the 1907 version of *Ben-Hur* to *Gladiator*, released in 2000, have depicted Rome in a negative light. Do you think Rome received fair treatment in *Ben-Hur*? Why or why not? *Possible answers: Some students will argue that the film depictions of Rome have been fair because as an imperial power, Rome mistreated many people. Others will argue that Hollywood has been unfair by ignoring Rome's many contributions to human history.*

## GUIDED VIEWING ACTIVITY ANSWERS

1. The chains are intended to prevent them from abandoning their oars during battle.
2. After it is rammed, the ship takes on water and begins to sink.
3. They use a row of metal dolphins. After each lap, a dolphin is pointed downward.
4. His chariot has blades that destroy the wheels of other racers.
5. Judah is crowned the victor.

**Ben-Hur**

# Guided Viewing Activity
## Rome

### SCENE 1

1. Why are the galley slaves chained?

_____

_____

_____

2. How does ramming damage the ship?

_____

_____

_____

### SCENE 2

3. How do the Romans show that a lap has been completed in the chariot race?

_____

_____

_____

4. How does Messala cheat in the race?

_____

_____

_____

5. Who wins the chariot race?

_____

_____

_____

# Analyzing Primary Sources

These readings by Roman writers discuss two institutions—slavery and bloody public entertainments—that appear in *Ben-Hur*,

**Source 1: From a Roman play in which a slave talks about his life**

> "Stripes [wounds], fetters, the mill, weariness, hunger, bitter cold—fine pay for idleness. That's what I'm mightily afraid of. Surely, then, it's much better to be good than to be bad. I don't mind tongue lashings, but I do hate real floggings."
>
> —Plautus, *Menaechmi,* Act V, Scene 4, c. AD 200

**For Discussion**  Do you think the life of Roman slaves was accurately portrayed in *Ben-Hur*?

**Source 2: From two critics of Roman society**

> "For the people—who once conferred *imperium* [power], symbols of office, legions, everything—now hold themselves in check and anxiously desire only two things, the grain dole [free food] and chariot races in the Circus."
>
> —Juvenal, *Satires* 10.77–81, first century AD

> "It was really mere butchery . . . The slayer was kept fighting until he could be slain. 'Kill him! flog him! burn him alive!' was the cry: 'Why is he such a coward? Why won't he rush on the steel? Why does he fall so meekly? Why won't he die willingly?' Unhappy that I am, how have I deserved that I must look on such a scene as this? Do not, my Lucilius, attend the games, I pray you. Either you will be corrupted by the multitude, or, if you show disgust, be hated by them. So stay away."
>
> —Seneca the Younger, *Epistles 7*, first century AD

**For Discussion**  Do the views of Seneca, who was writing about the gladiatorial games, and Juvenal surprise you? Why or why not? How do their views compare to what you saw of the Roman people in *Ben-Hur*?

## ANSWERS

**Source 1** *Possible answer: Although the slaves shown in Ben-Hur were galley slaves, their treatment was similarly harsh.*

**Source 2** *Possible answers: Students may be surprised to learn that some Romans criticized chariot races and gladiatorial games. Most students will note that the public's enthusiasm for entertainment, which the writers criticized, was shown in the film.*

# Movie Guide
## Early Russia

> 1938; Sergei Eisenstein, Director; Starring Nikolai Cherkasov, Nikolai Okhlopkov, Andrei Abrikosov, Dmitri Orlov, and Vasili Novikov
> 120 minutes, not rated, available on videotape and DVD, black and white

## WHY WATCH THIS MOVIE?

The highlight of *Alexander Nevsky* is a battle between Russian forces and German invaders fought on ice in 1242. Sergei Eisenstein, who is still regarded as one of the world's most brilliant film directors, shot the battle scene during a hot summer. The ice is in fact a mixture of chalk and salt.

The hero of the film is Prince Alexander. In 1240 the prince had successfully defended the city of Novgorod from a Swedish attack. He left Novgorod after a dispute with city leaders but returned the following year to defend it from German invaders. The battle on the ice took place on Lake Piepus in April 1242. The Russian victory ended the German threat.

Eisenstein filmed *Alexander Nevsky* at a time when the rising power of Nazi Germany posed a serious threat to Soviet security. The film was an immediate hit with the Russian public—children bought thousands of paper clips to make chain mail like that worn by Prince Alexander. Pleased with the movie, Soviet premier Joseph Stalin awarded the Order of Lenin to Eisenstein and lead actor Nikolai Cherkasov. In late 1939, however, *Alexander Nevsky* became unavailable to the public. The Soviet Union had signed a nonaggression pact with Germany, and all films critical of the nation's new ally were withdrawn from circulation. This turn of events did not last. After Germany invaded the Soviet Union in 1941, Stalin ordered *Alexander Nevsky* to be shown again in theaters to build support for the war effort.

## THE SCENES

**Scene 1** (from 00:17:00 to 00:22:00, 5 minutes) opens with a wounded messenger arriving in Novgorod. He announces that the Germans have destroyed nearby Pskov and are marching toward the city. The assembled crowd is fearful, but the merchants who rule Novgorod argue that the Germans can be paid not to attack. The crowd angrily accuses the merchants of being disloyal to the homeland. Ignat, a maker of armor, rouses the crowd when he demands that Alexander be summoned to fight the Germans. City leaders have no desire to see Alexander return, but the crowd wins the day.

**Scene 2** (from 00:50:50 to 01:24:00, 33 minutes) starts when Alexander rejects the advice of his men and formulates a plan to fight the Germans on the lake ice. The battle begins the next day. The Germans form a wedge and hammer the Russian center. Alexander waits and then has his army attack the Germans on their flanks. A mighty battle ensues. The Germans flee in panic, but many drown as their heavy armor drags them under the ice.

## DISCUSSION QUESTIONS BASED ON THE SCENES

1. Why do the people of Novgorod disagree with the merchants who lead the city? What does this scene reveal about the filmmaker's attitude toward merchants and people who make a great deal of money? *Possible answers: Students should note that the merchants are interested only in their own well-being and do not express any love for their homeland. The people, however, regard the arrival of the Germans as a death sentence. This scene is very critical of merchants, who are portrayed as selfish and disloyal. (Students who are familiar with communist economic ideas may note that this criticism would have reflected the Soviet government's attitude toward capitalism and capitalists.)*

Teacher's Guide to Analyzing Movies

2. How does Eisenstein portray the Russians? How does he depict the Germans? How do the director's choices influence the audience's reactions to events in the film? *Possible answers: Nevsky and his followers are depicted as brave defenders of the homeland. Vasily takes delight in battling the enemy, and a Russian woman can be seen fighting alongside the men, revealing the depth of the Russian commitment to the homeland. The Germans are sinister, often faceless beings who are a menacing foe. By making the Russians empathetic human beings and the Germans into demonic creatures, he ensures that his audience will cheer when the Russians are victorious.*

## WHAT CAN STUDENTS LEARN FROM THESE SCENES?

Students learn about the history of Russia in the 1200s, because the events presented in the motion picture are generally accurate. Prince Alexander did save Novgorod from the Germans. The tactics portrayed in the battle, including that of allowing the Germans to use their wedge attack before the Russians rushed their flanks, are also correct. However, teachers might lead students in a discussion of the portrayal of the Germans and the intense nationalism depicted in the film, which Eisenstein created without much historical evidence.

## WHAT HAPPENS NEXT? HOW DOES THE STORY END?

Alexander and his men return to Novgorod with their German prisoners. Alexander shows mercy by sparing soldiers who were forced to fight for the Germans. He promises to ransom the German officers. However, he allows a mob to murder a Russian who aided the Germans. The film ends with Alexander declaring, "He who comes to us sword in hand shall perish by the sword. On that our Russian land will forever take its stand."

## IF YOUR CLASS WATCHES THE ENTIRE FILM

Historians agree that *Alexander Nevsky* is largely accurate in its portrayal of the battle on the ice. However, they note that the film's intense nationalism and anti-German tone is more about events in 1938 than in 1242. Do you think that film directors should use historical films to comment on contemporary events? Do you think that popular films should be used for propaganda purposes by governments? *Possible answers: Some students might argue that all historical films contain some elements that relate to current events. Others might claim that allowing contemporary issues to intrude on a film's plot distorts the historical record. Students will offer different responses to the issue of propaganda, with some rejecting such efforts and others applauding them if the cause is considered a good one.*

## GUIDED VIEWING ACTIVITY ANSWERS

1. The crowd panics when they learn of the devastation of Pskov.

2. The merchants claim that the Germans can be bribed into not attacking Novgorod.

3. He vows that the Germans will never set foot on Russian soil, so he must fight them on the lake.

4. A German dressed in black robes plays strange music on a pipe organ. The Germans wear odd and terrifying helmets into battle.

5. The sledges prevent his men from retreating.

Teacher's Guide to Analyzing Movies

**_Alexander Nevsky_**                 Guided Viewing Activity
                                            **Early Russia**

## SCENE 1

1. How does the crowd react to the news that the city of Pskov has fallen to the Germans?

   _____

   _____

   _____

2. How do the merchants plan to halt the German invasion?

   _____

   _____

   _____

## SCENE 2

3. Why does Alexander decide to fight the Germans on the ice?

   _____

   _____

   _____

4. How does the film director make the Germans appear to be evil and menacing?

   _____

   _____

   _____

5. Why does Vasily place sledges behind his men?

   _____

   _____

   _____

# Analyzing Primary and Secondary Sources

These excerpts may enhance your viewing of *Alexander Nevsky*.

## Source 1: From a history of Russia, 1984

"Although the Mongol invasion failed to reach Novgorod, the principality together with other Russian lands submitted to the khan. In fact, the great warrior Alexander Nevskii [Nevsky] himself instituted this policy of co-operation with the Mongols, becoming a favorite of the khan and thus the grand prince of Russia from 1252 until his death in 1263. Alexander Nevskii acted as he did because of a simple and sound reason: he considered resistance to the Mongols hopeless. And it was especially because of his humble submission to the khan and his consequent ability to preserve the principality of Novgorod as well as some other Russian lands from ruin that the Orthodox Church canonized Alexander Nevskii."

—Nicholas V. Riasanovsky, *A History of Russia*, 1984

**For Discussion** How does this aspect of Alexander Nevsky's character contrast with his portrayal in the film? How would emphasis on the Mongol issue have affected the film?

## Source 2: From the rules for Teutonic Knights, 1264

"How the brethren shall set people a good example. Whenever the brethren are travelling or going against the enemy or on other business, since they display outwardly by the Cross the sign of meekness and of the Order, they shall strive to show people, by examples of good deeds and useful words, that God is with and within them."

—*The Rule and Statutes of the Teutonic Knights,* translated by Indrikis Sterns

**For Discussion** How does this description of the Teutonic Knights' behavior contrast with how they appear in *Alexander Nevsky*? Why did the director choose to show the knights as he did?

## ANSWERS

**Source 1** *Possible answers: In the film, Alexander Nevsky is shown as a valiant leader rather than a practical politician. Emphasis on his dealings with the Mongols might have detracted from the heroic portrayal.*

**Source 2** *Possible answers: The Rule requires the Knights to be virtuous, in contrast to the brutishness they show in the film. The director had to portray them as faceless and threatening so that they would fit with his goal of demonizing the Germans in his propagandistic film.*

> 1964; Peter Glenville, Director; Starring Richard Burton, Peter O'Toole, John Gielgud, Donald Wolfit, Marita Hunt, Pamela Brown, and Felix Aylmer
>
> 148 minutes, not rated, available on videotape and DVD, color
>
> This activity applies to the 1964 film. Motion pictures with the same title were released in 1910 and 1923.

## WHY WATCH THIS MOVIE?

At least since the reign of Charlemagne, there had been tensions between European rulers and church leaders. *Becket* explores that tension as it played out in the complex and ultimately tragic relationship between Henry II and Thomas Becket. A great-grandson of William the Conqueror, Henry became king of England in 1154. Among his many accomplishments was strengthening England's court and financial systems.

To assist him in his efforts, Henry appointed his close friend Thomas Becket to the position of chancellor. This job combined the duties of a personal chaplain and a secretary. Becket excelled at the job, helping Henry make the English monarchy more powerful. Henry's increase in power worried many church officials. They did not believe that the king held any power over the church, and they loudly opposed many of Henry's actions. In 1162 Henry named Becket archbishop of Canterbury, the highest position in the church in England. Henry wanted to have a strong ally within the church. However, his plan backfired. Becket took his new job seriously. In time, he became more loyal to the church than to the king.

Based on a play by Jean Anouilh, the 1964 motion picture won three Academy Awards. However, it does contain several historical inaccuracies. For example, Thomas Becket was a Norman, but throughout the film he is identified as a Saxon. In early scenes Becket is portrayed as living a wild life, but the real Becket held fast to a vow of chastity taken in his youth.

## THE SCENES

**Scene 1** (from 00:16:24 to 00:21:56, 5 minutes) opens as Henry tells a group of churchmen that he intends to make war on the king of France and that they must contribute money or troops for the cause. The churchmen protest that since the days of William the Conqueror they have been exempt from such a requirement. As the newly appointed chancellor, Becket stands by the king.

**Scene 2** (from 01:59:00 to 02:05:35, 6 minutes) takes place as Becket has become archbishop of Canterbury and has defied Henry on several issues. Most important, he has excommunicated a prominent noble and refused to turn over priests to be tried in the king's courts instead of in church courts. Charged with a number of crimes he has not committed, Becket fled to France to escape arrest. The archbishop and the king, once close friends but now bitterly opposed, meet on a beach in northern France to discuss their differences.

## DISCUSSION QUESTIONS BASED ON THE SCENES

1. In Scene 1, Henry says he has hired Swiss soldiers to fight for him. What might this indicate about the king's resources at the time? How does Henry's problem contribute to his conflict with the churchmen? *Possible answers: Henry has limited resources, not only of cash but also of fighting men. Previous kings had more money and men and did not have to ask the church for cash. Henry's lack of both set the conflict into motion.*

2. How does Becket react to the churchmen in Scene 1? How has his attitude changed by Scene 2? What might happen next? *Possible answers: In Scene 1, Becket tells the churchmen that they must obey their king's orders. In Scene 2, he supports the church's position and refuses to give in to the king's requests. Since neither man gives in, the scene is set for a violent confrontation.*

## WHAT CAN STUDENTS LEARN FROM THESE SCENES?

Students learn the general appearance of a medieval castle, armor, and clothing. (However, if you show scenes that include the king's wife and mother, note that their clothing is highly inaccurate for the period. Their elaborate styles date from the 1400s.) More important, students should understand the importance of the clash between the state, in the form of the king, and the church. The rift between Becket and Henry II represents the first time that such a conflict became a major issue for the English monarchy. In fact, similar controversies would mark the reigns of many kings and queens throughout Europe in the following centuries. For example, students may already know about King Henry VIII, who broke completely with the Roman Catholic Church in a power struggle with the pope. In the process, Henry VIII created the Church of England. Issues of church and state were fundamental to our country's creation and were eventually embodied in our constitution's Bill of Rights. Moreover, separation of church and state continues to affect political matters in our own day.

## WHAT HAPPENS NEXT? HOW DOES THE STORY END?

Becket returns to England and resumes his duties as archbishop. The king plans to have his son Henry crowned as his co-ruler, but at York instead of Canterbury, the traditional place for coronations. This switch is intended to rebuke Becket for his refusal to give in to the king. Finally, the king asks a group of knights, "Will no one rid me of this meddlesome priest?" (However, there is no historical evidence that Henry ever spoke these actual words.) The knights assume that Henry wants Becket killed. They kill him in Canterbury Cathedral.

## IF YOUR CLASS WATCHES THE ENTIRE FILM

A major source of tension between Henry II and church leaders was the role of ecclesiastical courts. The church claimed the right to try members of the clergy in its own court system. Henry regarded these courts as a limit on his authority and demanded that clergy accused of crimes be tried in civil courts. Initially agreeing with Henry, Becket later ardently defended the ecclesiastical courts. How does the film explain Becket's change of heart? Do you find this a believable explanation? *Possible answers: The film portrays Becket's newfound respect for the church as the result of his search for honor in life. Some students might find this portrayal convincing, whereas others might wonder if Becket found that his new role gave him great power and that wielding power was really what he wanted.*

## GUIDED VIEWING ACTIVITY ANSWERS

1. Becket is surprised and uncertain if he can handle the position.

2. Henry is rude and disrespectful.

3. Becket sides with the king in this scene.

4. He will not discuss his decision to make Becket archbishop.

5. He does so because in the past the two men had been friends.

***Becket***                                  Guided Viewing Activity
                                              **The Middle Ages**

## SCENE 1

1. How does Becket respond to the announcement that he will become chancellor?

_____

_____

_____

2. How does Henry treat the archbishop?

_____

_____

_____

3. Is Becket loyal to the church or to King Henry II?

_____

_____

_____

## SCENE 2

4. What topic does Henry refuse to discuss with Becket?

_____

_____

_____

5. Why does the king allow Becket to return to England?

_____

_____

_____

## Analyzing Primary Sources

This account from the only eyewitness to Thomas Becket's murder may enhance your viewing of *Becket*.

**From a clerk who was severely wounded trying to save Becket**

"When the holy archbishop entered the cathedral the monks who were glorifying God abandoned vespers . . . and ran to their father whom they had heard was dead but they saw alive and unharmed. They hastened to close the doors of the church in order to bar the enemies from slaughtering the bishop, but the wondrous athlete turned toward them and ordered that the doors be opened. 'It is not proper,' he said, 'that a house of prayer, a church of Christ, be made a fortress since although it is not shut up, it serves as a fortification for his people; we will triumph over the enemy through suffering rather than by fighting—and we come to suffer, not to resist'. . .

"Those knights . . . exclaimed in a rage: 'Where is Thomas Becket, traitor of the king and kingdom?'. . . 'Here I am, not a traitor of the king but a priest; why do you seek me? . . . Here I am ready to suffer in the name of He who redeemed me with His blood; God forbid that I should flee on account of your swords or that I should depart from righteousness'. . .

"But during all these incredible things the martyr displayed the virtue of perseverance. Neither his hand nor clothes indicated that he had opposed a murderer—as is often the case in human weakness; nor when stricken did he utter a word, nor did he let out a cry or a sigh, or a sign signaling any kind of pain; instead he held still the head that he had bent toward the unsheathed swords."

—Edward Grim,
*Vita S. Thomae, Cantuariensis Archepiscopi et Martyris,* c. 1180

**For Discussion** According to Grim, how did Becket meet his death? Why do you think Becket acted as he did? How does the portrayal of Becket in the movie compare to how he is portrayed in this account? Could Grim's version of the murder be inaccurate or exaggerated?

## ANSWERS

*Possible answers: Becket met his death calmly and bravely and even seemed to welcome it. He may have realized that his death would actually enhance his argument against the monarchy and shame the king. Grim's portrayal supports the portrayal of Becket in Scene 2. Although he was an eyewitness, Grim could still have presented an inaccurate or exaggerated version, because he clearly admired Becket.*

# Movie Guide
## Early Japan

---

1980; Jerry London, Director; Starring Richard Chamberlain, Toshiro Mifune, Yoko Shimada, Frankie Sakia, Alan Badel, Damien Thomas, and Michael Hordern

547 minutes, not rated, available on videotape and DVD, color

---

## WHY WATCH THIS MOVIE?

*Shogun* portrays the culture and politics of samurai society in Japan of the 1600s. The historical setting is a conflict between two daimyo, both of whom want to become shogun. The character of Lord Toranaga, one of the daimyo, is based on the life of Tokugawa Ieyasu, who became shogun in 1603.

*Shogun* was broadcast in the United States in 1980 as a television mini-series. The program was based on James Clavell's popular novel of the same title, which sold over 6 million copies in the 1970s. Clavell began the novel after reading about the adventures of William Adams in one of his daughter's schoolbooks. Adams, an English sailor who arrived in Japan in 1600, served as an adviser to Tokugawa Ieyasu. Clavell transformed the historical Adams into the fictional John Blackthorne, who is shipwrecked in Japan and eventually rises to the position of samurai. Blackthorne's perceptions of Japanese society and his dealings with the daimyo Toranaga are the focus of the mini-series.

For many Americans, the 1980 mini-series served as an introduction to Japanese history and culture. Although *Shogun* is a heavily fictionalized account of historical events, the producers strove for accuracy in their depictions of costumes and customs. Thus, students can learn much about Japan from this program.

## THE SCENES

**Scene 1** (from 00:09:10 to 00:21:40, 12 minutes) begins with Englishman John Blackthorne awakening in a strange house after the Dutch ship he pilots has struck a reef. He quickly realizes he is in Japan, a destination he has long sought. He encounters unfriendly Japanese men occupying his ship and a hostile Portuguese priest on the beach. The local samurai grants Blackthorne permission to walk around the village, but shocks the Englishman when he executes a disobedient servant. *Note: This scene contains a beheading, but it happens very quickly, and the violence is not graphic.*

**Scene 2** (from 04:04:30 to 04:15:00, 8 minutes) starts with Blackthorne living in a village under the control of Lord Yabu. If the villagers do not succeed in teaching Blackthorne the Japanese language within six months, Lord Yabu has decreed that all the villagers will be executed. Blackthorne and Mariko, his secret lover, meet with Yabu, and Blackthorne asks him to lift the decree. When Yabu refuses, Blackthorne threatens to commit seppuku, or ritual suicide. At the last minute, Yabu and his aide prevent Blackthorne from stabbing himself. The Englishman realizes that he is in some ways becoming like the Japanese.

## DISCUSSION QUESTIONS BASED ON THE SCENES

1. What does Scene 1 reveal about the Japanese perceptions of foreigners? What does it reveal about the power of the samurai? *Possible answers: The Japanese are suspicious of the foreigners, but have given the pilot some freedom. In addition, the Portuguese priest clearly has influenced the Japanese, as revealed by the cross on the wall of the house in which Blackthorne wakes. The samurai's power seems absolute, in that even the slightest hint of disobedience results in a quick death that elicits no objections from the villagers.*

---

Teacher's Guide to Analyzing Movies

2. What does Scene 2 reveal about the importance of honor in Japanese society? *Possible answer: Students might note that although Yabu does not want Blackthorne to die, he accepts the argument that dishonor and shame might merit suicide.*

## WHAT CAN STUDENTS LEARN FROM THESE SCENES?

Students learn about Japanese culture in the 1600s. The mini-series offers insight into the dress, housing, and social customs of the Japanese. Students can learn about the role of honor and ritual in Japanese society, as revealed in the scene involving seppuku, or ritual suicide. Finally, *Shogun* offers insights into the complicated relationships between the Japanese and Europeans during the Age of Exploration.

## WHAT HAPPENS NEXT? HOW DOES THE STORY END?

Blackthorne becomes close to Lord Toranaga, who makes the Englishman a samurai. Blackthorne is in constant danger, however, because Toranaga's rival, Lord Ishido, regards the English pilot as a threat to his own ambition to become shogun. In addition, the Portuguese wish to eliminate Blackthorne because he has learned of the lucrative trade monopoly they have established with Japan. Murder, mystery, and complicated court intrigue drive the plot. By the program's end, Lord Toranaga has become shogun, and Blackthorne has become an honored friend. However, Toranaga will destroy any ships that Blackthorne builds so that the Englishman can never leave Japan.

## IF YOUR CLASS WATCHES THE ENTIRE FILM

Filmmakers often use the convention of a shipwrecked or isolated westerner to explore the customs and cultures of other societies. Examples range from *Shogun* to the 2003 motion picture *The Last Samurai.* Some film critics have complained that this convention distorts other societies and cultures because it makes them appear too strange and mysterious. Do you agree with this criticism? What scenes in *Shogun* might you rewrite to make Japanese cultural values more understandable to western audiences? *Possible answers: Student responses will vary. Students should discuss the benefits and challenges of the "isolated westerner" as a plot device. They should then identify specific scenes in* Shogun *that left them confused or uncertain about Japanese customs and suggest ways that those scenes could be improved.*

## GUIDED VIEWING ACTIVITY ANSWERS

1. The Jesuit is hostile, accusing Blackthorne of being a pirate and then condemning him to hell.

2. The samurai beheads the villager.

3. Yabu argues that the villagers mean nothing.

4. Blackthorne argues that he is shamed and dishonored, and cannot bear to have the fate of the village on his conscience.

5. He realizes that he has adopted some of the mindset of the Japanese with whom he has been living.

*Shogun* 

# Guided Viewing Activity

## Early Japan

## SCENE 1

1. How does the Jesuit priest treat Blackthorne?

_____

_____

_____

2. What does the samurai do to the villager who refuses to bow?

_____

_____

_____

## SCENE 2

3. How does Lord Yabu regard the villagers he has threatened with execution?

_____

_____

_____

4. Why does Blackthorne threaten to commit suicide?

_____

_____

_____

5. What realization does Blackthorne come to after he is stopped from killing himself?

_____

_____

_____

_____

## Analyzing Primary and Secondary Sources

These passages may enhance your viewing of *Shogun*:

**Source 1: From a letter from William Adams, the inspiration for Blackthorne in the film, to his wife about his meeting with Tokugawa Ieyasu, whom he describes as a king**

"In the end, there came one that could speak Portuguese. By him, the king demanded of me of what land I was, and what moved us to come to his land, being so far off. I showed unto him the name of our country, and that our land had long sought out the East Indies, and desired friendship with all kinds and potentates in way of merchandise, having in our land diverse commodities, which these lands had not . . . He asked me diverse other questions of things of religion, and many other things: As what way we came to the country. Having a chart [map] of the whole world, I showed him, through the Strait of Magellan. At which he wondered, and thought me to lie. Thus, from one thing to another, I abode with him till midnight."

—William Adams, 1600

**For Discussion** Why was Adams's ship in Japanese waters? What do we learn about the Japanese knowledge of geography?

**Source 2: From a history of the samurai, on the subject of suicide**

"In fact the samurai tradition of suicide to save one's honour may have lost Japan many fine generals who would otherwise have lived to fight another day. It is instructive to look at [Korean] Admiral Yi Sun Sin, who was utterly disgraced, tortured and imprisoned . . . Had Yi been a Japanese admiral he would certainly have committed suicide, whereas Yi withstood all his degradation and returned to attack the Japanese again in 1598."

—S. R. Turnbull, *The Samurai: A Military History*, 1977

**For Discussion** Why would a society develop such a horrific tradition as suicide, when it poses such a risk for the country as a whole?

## ANSWERS

**Source 1** *Possible answers: Adams's ship was seeking trade. The Japanese had little knowledge of world geography, as shown by Tokugawa's reaction to the map.*
**Source 2** *Possible answers: Students may suggest that, since the threat to Japan from outsiders seemed minimal, the desire of the ruling samurai class to maintain discipline took precedence over the need to keep capable soldiers who could help defend the country.*

Teacher's Guide to Analyzing Movies

1986; Roland Joffe, Director; Starring Robert De Niro, Jeremy Irons, Ray McAnally, Aidan Quinn, Chuck Low, and Ronald Pickup

126 minutes, rated PG, available on videotape and DVD, color

## WHY WATCH THIS MOVIE?

*The Mission* captures the sometimes tragic consequences of European colonization in the Americas. Set near the border of Paraguay and Uruguay in the 1750s, the film explores the fate of the Guaraní people who lived and worked in Jesuit missions. According to the terms of a 1750 treaty, control of territory around the missions shifted from Spain to Portugal. Because the Portuguese allowed for the enslavement of the Indians while the Spanish officially opposed it, the future of the mission's people was in doubt. In the film, Cardinal Altamirano represents the interests of the Roman Catholic Church. He must determine if the missions should receive Spanish protection. Spain and Portugal both prefer that Altamirano transfer the missions to the Portuguese in keeping with the terms of the treaty. The cardinal realizes that if he does so, the Guaraní are doomed. However, if he chooses to protect the missions, he will anger European leaders already hostile to the interests of the church. It is around this agonizing decision that the film is constructed.

To add dramatic tension to the tale, screenwriter Robert Bolt created two fictional Jesuit priests. Father Gabriel, of whom the Guaraní are very fond, is committed to peace and rejects all violence. Former mercenary and slave trader Rodrigo Mendoza disagrees. He sees violence as the only means to protect the Indians to whom he has dedicated his life.

*The Mission* was released in the mid-1980s, a time of turmoil in Latin America. Many priests who opposed their government and championed the poor were persecuted, and some priests were murdered. Thus, *The Mission* was not merely a historical study; it touched on an issue that was important and all too real in some countries.

## THE SCENES

**Scene 1** (from 00:54:28 to 01:02:22, 8 minutes) opens with Cardinal Altamirano listening to a debate between Cabeza, a Spaniard who wants the missions closed, and Father Gabriel, a defender of the Guaraní. Father Mendoza insults Cabeza, who uses the situation to embarrass the Jesuits. Later, Altamirano explains to Father Gabriel the complicated circumstances surrounding his visit.

**Scene 2** (from 01:17:40 to 01:26:15, 9 minutes) starts with Cardinal Altamirano visiting a mission. Deeply moved by the beauty of the community, he nonetheless announces that the Indians must abandon it. The Indians reject his order and vow to defend their homes. Altamirano commands the Jesuits to depart and explains to Gabriel that the survival of the Jesuits in Europe requires the sacrifice of the missions.

## DISCUSSION QUESTIONS BASED ON THE SCENES

1. What does Scene 1 reveal about differing European attitudes toward the Indians? How might these viewpoints have influenced colonization? *Possible answers: The Jesuits regard them as human beings who can be taught and whose souls must be saved. The Spanish and Portuguese officials dismiss the indigenous people as animals who must be subdued with force. These differing perspectives complicated the process of colonization because the Europeans had different goals for the lands they colonized.*

2. How might the Guaraní have understood the events portrayed in these scenes? *Possible answer: Unfamiliar with the complexity of church-state relationships in Europe, the Guaraní might have based their understanding just on the actions of the Europeans in their midst. In the end, they probably would have distrusted the Europeans, who seem violent in some cases and unreliable in others.*

## WHAT CAN STUDENTS LEARN FROM THESE SCENES?

Students learn that the relations between the Roman Catholic Church and the governments of European nations were complex. Although Spain relied on missionary activity to advance the process of colonization, the goals of the church and the state conflicted at times. In addition, the students gain some insight into the difficulties Indians faced in adapting to the presence of colonizers. Some, as represented by Father Gabriel, treated them with mercy and justice. Others, as represented by Cabeza, saw them as obstacles or as potential laborers to be exploited. The indigenous people had no control over European politics and so had great difficulty in protecting their homelands and their cultures.

## WHAT HAPPENS NEXT? HOW DOES THE STORY END?

Both Gabriel and Mendoza remain at the mission, Gabriel to minister to the Guaraní, Mendoza to lead them in armed resistance. Portuguese troops attack and begin a massacre. Mendoza is shot. As he lies dying, he sees Gabriel performing mass. Gabriel is murdered, too, and the mission is swept by flames. The film ends with a group of orphaned children leaving the mission in a canoe and heading toward the jungle.

## IF YOUR CLASS WATCHES THE ENTIRE FILM

The fictional priests in *The Mission* both fail. Mendoza tries to defend the mission through the use of violence, but he and the Indians are killed by the Portuguese. Gabriel believes that violence is wrong and that Christian love is the only path that the Jesuits can follow. He also dies as the mission is destroyed. The filmmaker's creation of these characters makes for great drama, but do you think it offers a simplistic portrayal of choices that people must make? Should the filmmakers have offered the perspectives of other people involved in the story? *Possible answers: Some students will note that films must create dramatic tension in order to capture an audience's attention. They might also argue that a motion picture has a limited amount of time to present a complicated story. Others will argue that additional alternatives, perhaps offered from a Guaraní character, would make the story more complex and interesting.*

## GUIDED VIEWING ACTIVITY ANSWERS

1. He argues that they do not regret their sins and respond only to force.
2. Cabeza has claimed that there are no Indian slaves in Spanish territory.
3. He is impressed by its beauty and by the peaceful nature of the people there.
4. The Guaraní do not want to leave their homes in the mission, and argue that the cardinal does not know God's will.
5. He orders them to leave the mission.

Teacher's Guide to Analyzing Movies

**The Mission**

Guided Viewing Activity

**Exploration and Colonization**

**SCENE 1**

1. Why does Don Cabeza regard the Native Americans as animals?

_____

_____

_____

2. Why does Mendoza call Don Cabeza a liar?

_____

_____

_____

**SCENE 2**

3. What features of mission life impress Cardinal Altamirano?

_____

_____

_____

4. Why do the Guaraní reject the cardinal's decision regarding the mission?

_____

_____

_____

5. What does the cardinal order the Jesuits to do in this scene?

_____

_____

_____

## Analyzing Primary Sources

These passages may enhance your viewing of *The Mission*:

**Source 1: From an order by the king of Spain to officials in Mexico**

> "Juan de la Peña has reported to me saying that because the Indians of this province are not gathered into towns where they may be governed and controlled much harm is done. Many difficulties arise in their conversion because they are not taught to live under the control and ordered system leading to their salvation and welfare . . . I have therefore approved it, and do now command you to issue orders and instructions for gathering the Indians of that province who are wandering in the mountains into towns. Here they may . . . be more easily taught the Catholic religion."
>
> —King Philip II, 1570

**For Discussion** What bias does the king's order display? How might the Indians to whom he refers have seen his order? How do you think the king's attitude affected indigenous peoples throughout Spain's American colonies? How is his attitude reflected in the film?

**Source 2: From a Spaniard who sailed with explorer John Cabot in 1527**

> "There is yet another tribe, spread over a wide area, friendly to us, called Guarenís . . . They are hostile to all the other tribes, and exploit them. They are treacherous people, everything they do is by treachery
> . . . They bring down gold and silver in the form of plates, or as ear ornaments, or hatchets, which they use to clear the scrub for growing their crops. They are cannibals."
>
> —Luis Ramírez, quoted in *The Discovery of South America,* by J. H. Parry

**For Discussion** How does this description of the Guaraní compare to their portrayal in *The Mission*? What might account for the difference?

## ANSWERS

**Source 1** *Possible answers: The king's order reflects his bias that all people should live in towns and submit to his religion and government. The Indians probably saw the order as a puzzling and unwelcome violation of their traditional way of life. His attitude did affect people throughout the Americas, as many were mistreated and their native cultures destroyed. In the film, the officials who have no real concern for the Indians seem to hold similar views.*
**Source 2** *Possible answers: This description is more negative than the movie's portrayal. The difference may be because the 1527 account was inaccurate, because the Guaraní had changed by the time of the movie's events, or because the movie director wanted the audience to sympathize with the Guaraní. Students may suggest other explanations also.*

# *A Man For All Seasons*

> 1966; Fred Zimmerman, Director; Starring Paul Scofield, Wendy Hiller, Leo McKern, Robert Shaw, Orson Welles, Susannah York, and Vanessa Redgrave
>
> 120 minutes, not rated, available on videotape and DVD, color
>
> This activity applies to the 1966 original of the film. There is also a 1988 remake.

## WHY WATCH THIS MOVIE?

*A Man For All Seasons* powerfully portrays the battle between idealism and absolutism, focusing on the conflict between England's King Henry VIII and one of his most trusted advisers, Sir Thomas More, in the 1500s. The film's opening sequences set the stage by revealing the political intrigue surrounding the king's court. Cardinal Thomas Wolsey has failed to secure permission from the pope for Henry to divorce his wife, Catherine, and Wolsey dies in disgrace. Nonetheless, More believes that the king's decision to declare himself head of the Church of England in order to secure a divorce is an affront to God. Fully aware that his dedication to his faith may result in tragedy, More struggles to balance the demands of Henry with the dictates of the Roman Catholic Church. He hopes to find safety in the law, but a dramatic court scene reveals that Henry's earthly desires have corrupted the courts. More pays for his conscience with his life in an execution scene that concludes the motion picture.

*A Man For All Seasons* is based on a play of the same name written by Robert Bolt. The play was a success in London and New York, but there were doubts that a filmed version would be popular, as the play contains a great deal of dialogue, little action, and no romance. Yet the movie was a hit with the public, earning six Academy Awards, including Best Picture, Best Director, and Best Actor. The film was widely praised for its portrayal of a man who remained steadfast to what he thought was right and refused to back down in the face of tyranny, even though it cost him his life.

## THE SCENES

**Scene 1** (from 00:34:40 to 00:43:00, 8 minutes) shows Henry VIII and More conversing at More's Chelsea estate. Henry argues that his marriage to Catherine, the widow of his brother Arthur, is a sin and that he must have a divorce. More cannot bring himself to approve of the divorce even as Henry makes clear that he will not tolerate any opposition to his plans.

**Scene 2** (from 01:28:07 to 01:35:28, 7 minutes) opens with More having refused to take an oath acknowledging the Act of Succession, which recognizes King Henry VIII as the head of the Church of England. For his refusal, More has been imprisoned in the Tower of London. In this scene, a court of inquiry questions More regarding the oath. More displays his legal skills, declining to explain his reasons in order to avoid being accused of treason.

**Scene 3** (from 01:43:25 to 01:57:00, 14 minutes) is the dramatic climax of the motion picture. More appears before a court to defend himself against the charge of high treason. He believes that his silence on the issue of the oath affords him legal protection. However, Richard Rich commits perjury, claiming that More told him that Henry could not be head of the church. More's case is lost, and the court sentences him to death.

## DISCUSSION QUESTIONS BASED ON THE SCENES

1. How does King Henry treat More during their discussion in the garden? How does More respond to Henry's behavior? What does this scene reveal about the relationship between the two men? *Possible answers: Henry flatters and then bullies More in an effort to secure his support. More is deeply troubled but does not offer to help the king. Henry admires More but does not respect his opinions, demanding total loyalty. More is loyal to the king and does not know how to meet his demands yet remain true to his beliefs.*

2. What would the movie have been like had it been told from the perspective of Henry VIII? *Possible answer: More might have been portrayed as an ungrateful subject whose actions undermined the authority of the Crown.*

## WHAT CAN STUDENTS LEARN FROM THESE SCENES?

Students learn that the monarch had considerable power in England at this time and that the personality of the ruler affected the lives of everyone in the nation. The members of the court of inquiry support the king even though one of them does not understand the subtleties of the arguments presented. More wishes to serve his king but pays with his life. Students will also learn that justice can be denied through the corrupt behavior of an individual such as Richard Rich, whose perjury leads to More's execution. Finally, students learn how closely debates over religious beliefs were connected to political concerns.

## WHAT HAPPENS NEXT? HOW DOES THE STORY END?

More accepts the sentence of death with dignity. The final scene shows him in brief conversation with the executioner. An upraised ax appears on the screen, followed by a dull thud. A narrator concludes with a brief discussion of the fates of key characters in the tale.

## IF YOUR CLASS WATCHES THE ENTIRE FILM

Some film historians consider *A Man For All Seasons* to be a great motion picture. Others argue that even though many scenes are historically accurate, the film does not show the real Thomas More, who was not tolerant of religious beliefs other than his own. Do you think the film's message is weakened if its portrayal of More is historically inaccurate? Why or why not? *Possible answers: Some students will state that films cannot be entirely accurate and allow filmmakers some license. Others may argue that the film cannot be trusted because of its inaccuracies and that making More a hero for his uncompromising adherence to his ideals must be questioned.*

## GUIDED VIEWING ACTIVITY ANSWERS

1. More knows the king wrote the music, so he compliments it while admitting he does not know much about music.

2. More appears physically exhausted.

3. He consistently refuses to provide an explanation.

4. More's books are taken away from him.

5. They do not discuss the matter at all but present their verdict immediately.

## *A Man For All Seasons*

## Guided Viewing Activity

### The Reformation in England

**SCENE 1**

  1. How does More respond to Henry's question regarding the music being played in the garden?

  _____

  _____

  _____

  2. How does More look when he is brought before the court of inquiry?

  _____

  _____

  _____

**SCENE 2**

  3. How does More respond to the demands that he explain his refusal to take the oath?

  _____

  _____

  _____

  4. How does the court of inquiry punish More for not cooperating?

  _____

  _____

  _____

**SCENE 3**

  5. How long does the jury discuss the charges against More?

  _____

  _____

  _____

Teacher's Guide to Analyzing Movies

## Analyzing Primary Sources

These quotations from Sir Thomas More's son-in-law may enhance your viewing of *A Man For All Seasons*. Both quotations are from *The Life of Sir Thomas More* by William Roper. Although Roper wrote the biography in about 1555, it was not published until 1626.

**Source 1: From a reported conversation between Roper and More**

"'Now would to God, so Roper, upon condition three things were well established in Christendom I were put in a sack, and here presently cast into the Thames . . . The first is, that whereas the most part of Christian princes be at mortal wars, they were at universal peace. The second, that where the Church of Christ is at this present sore afflicted with many heresies and errors, it were well settled in an uniformity of religion. The third, that where the King's matter of his marriage is now come into question, it were to the glory of God and quietness of all parties brought to a good conclusion.'"

**For Discussion** For what does More wish in this passage? What does More say he could accept if his wishes were granted?

**Source 2: From Alice More, the wife of Sir Thomas, visiting him in prison**

"'What the good year, Mr. More,' quoth she, 'I marvel that you, that have been always hitherunto taken for so wise a man, will now so play the fool to lie here in this close filthy prison, and be content to be shut up among mice and rats, when you might be abroad at your liberty . . . if you would but do as all the bishops and best learned of this Realm have done. And seeing you have at Chelsea a right fair house, your library, your books, your gallery, your garden, your orchards, and all necessaries so handsomely about you . . . I muse what a God's name you mean here still thus fondly to tarry.'"

**For Discussion** Do you have any sympathy for Alice More? Why or why not?

## ANSWERS

**Source 1** *Possible answers: More wishes for peace, the end of heresy in the church, and the settlement of the king's marriage. He promises he would allow himself to be put in a sack and thrown into the River Thames if those wishes were to be granted.*

**Source 2** *Possible answers: Some students may sympathize with "Mrs. Alice," as her husband calls her later in the quotation, because his protest may accomplish nothing and he has much to live for. Other students may criticize her for not supporting her husband's decision.*

1963; Luchino Visconti, Director; Starring Burt Lancaster, Claudia Cardinale, Alain Delon, Paolo Stoppa, Rina Morelli, and Terence Hill

161 minutes, not rated, available on DVD, color

Originally released in Italy as *Il Gattopardo*.

## WHY WATCH THIS MOVIE?

*The Leopard* is a study of an age-old human dilemma: How do we preserve those things in life that we love even as the world around us is rapidly changing? Prince Don Fabrizio Salina, a Sicilian aristocrat of the mid-1800s, faces this challenge in *The Leopard*. Fabrizio possesses great riches. His family has been part of the nobility for centuries, and he never doubts his right to command. Yet his world is threatened by *Il Risorgimento*, the political and military conflict that led to the unification of Italy.

Fabrizio is not a sympathetic character. He is rude to his servants and expects everyone around him, from his wife to the local priest, to do his bidding without question. Even as the spirit of republicanism and nationalism inspires the people of Sicily, Fabrizio is cynically focused on preserving his family's prestige and power.

To save his world, Fabrizio must abandon some of his principles. He is like a leopard, crafty and elusive in the pursuit of his prey. He pins his hopes for the future on Tancredi, his dynamic and charismatic nephew. Initially drawn to the revolutionary Giuseppe Garibaldi, Tancredi proves to be a man of little principle, switching sides according to his whims. To succeed in life, Tancredi needs a vast fortune, and he hopes to marry the beautiful and wealthy Angelica. Her father, Don Calogero, is a rich landlord who has no noble blood. Fabrizio finds him repugnant, but he approves the match nonetheless. Thus, to save his world, Fabrizio must destroy it, and the film hints but never reveals that the marriage represents the end of his way of life.

## THE SCENES

**Scene 1** (from 00:24:45 to 00:30:10, 5 minutes) depicts the battle of Palermo. Red Shirts under the command of Giuseppe Garibaldi attacked the Sicilian capital in late May 1860. This scene shows the women of Palermo attacking the mayor, a supporter of Bourbon rule. Fabrizio's nephew Tancredi is slightly injured by an exploding bomb.

**Scene 2** (from 00:37:00 to 00:44:20, 7 minutes) shows Fabrizio and his family paying a visit to a Sicilian town. The townspeople show their respect, and everyone attends a mass.

**Scene 3** (from 00:50:15 to 00:59:00, 10 minutes) opens with Don Calogero arriving at Fabrizio's palace for a dinner party. The family finds him to be an unmannered buffoon, but everyone is taken aback by the beauty of his daughter, Angelica. To impress her, Tancredi brags about his exploits with Garibaldi's army. The scene ends with Angelica laughing wildly, a breach of etiquette that offends the family.

## DISCUSSION QUESTIONS BASED ON THE SCENES

1. How does the director use the battle scene to portray the nationalist fervor that Garibaldi generated? *Possible answer: Students might contrast the Red Shirts with the Bourbon troops. Garibaldi's supporters wear vivid red tunics. They appear disorganized but are brave and successful in battle. The Bourbon troops are very organized but show no enthusiasm for their*

*cause. Most important, the people of Palermo rally to the Red Shirts, even attacking their mayor, a supporter of the Bourbons.*

2. In what ways does the movie offer insight into the world of aristocratic privilege? Why is Fabrizio's family so condescending to Don Calogero? *Possible answers: The scene in the Sicilian village reveals the respect that the nobles receive. The townspeople line the streets, and a band plays welcoming music. Men doff their hats. Family members are given seats of honor in the cathedral. The dinner party takes place in a room of extraordinary lavishness. Fabrizio's family mocks Don Calogero because he is unfamiliar with the rules of aristocratic behavior—rules learned from infancy and passed down through the generations.*

## WHAT CAN STUDENTS LEARN FROM THESE SCENES?

Students learn that the era of revolution in Europe threatened the world of aristocratic privilege. This privilege is reflected in the film's elaborate and ornate sets and the luxurious costumes. Students might also note the extraordinary deference shown to Fabrizio, although he does nothing to merit such respect in any of the scenes.

## WHAT HAPPENS NEXT? HOW DOES THE STORY END?

Fabrizio supports a fraudulent election because it serves his personal interests. He also decides that Tancredi must marry Angelica so that he will have the wealth and power to protect the family in the future. Tancredi abandons Garibaldi and joins the king's army. The final scene is a luxurious ballroom dance. In a sequence rich with symbols of decay and decline (for example, the painting depicting death), Fabrizio feels ill as he watches the dancers. Tancredi's rejection of republicanism is complete as he declares that rebels should be executed. In the film's final shot, Fabrizio walks home alone.

## IF YOUR CLASS WATCHES THE ENTIRE FILM

Film critics and film historians admire *The Leopard*, and the movie has influenced a generation of directors. The film succeeds because it relies upon subtlety and symbolism to portray the unraveling of Fabrizio's world. However, some viewers may find the motion picture frustrating because it has a slender plot and little action. If you were asked to remake *The Leopard*, what changes would you make? *Possible answers: Student answers will vary. Some students might want to relate the history of* Il Risorgimento *through the eyes of common people, or from the perspective of a soldier in Garibaldi's army. Others might continue the story of Fabrizio, showing what happened to the family.*

## GUIDED VIEWING ACTIVITY ANSWERS

1. The townspeople, led by the women, attack the mayor.

2. Tancredi is injured by a bomb that explodes near him in the street.

3. The townspeople line the streets, and as the family passes by, the men remove their hats.

4. He does not know how to wear the appropriate formal clothes.

5. They find her behavior offensive and leave the dinner table.

Teacher's Guide to Analyzing Movies

*The Leopard*                     # Guided Viewing Activity
## Italian Unification

## SCENE 1

1. Who attacks the mayor of Palermo (shown wearing a top hat)?

_____

_____

_____

2. How is Tancredi, the leader of the Red Shirts, wounded?

_____

_____

_____

## SCENE 2

3. How do the townspeople show their respect to Fabrizio and his family?

_____

_____

_____

## SCENE 3

4. Why does Fabrizio's family find Don Calogero so amusing?

_____

_____

_____

5. How does the family respond to Angelica's laughter?

_____

_____

_____

## Analyzing Primary Sources

This contemporary newspaper account may enhance your viewing of
*The Leopard.*

**From a reporter for *The Times* of London who traveled with Giuseppe Garibaldi during the liberation of Palermo, Sicily**

"Soon after my arrival Garibaldi made his appearance, and received his foreign visitors with that charming, quiet simplicity which characterizes him, lending himself with great complaisance to the invariably recurring demands of autographs, and answering the numerous questions which were naturally put to him. It was only after the departure of his guests that the General resumed business . . .

"Close to the Porta di Termini is the Vecchia Fiera—the old marketplace. This was the first point where Garibaldi stopped. One must know these Sicilians to have an idea of the frenzy, screaming, shouting, crying, and hugging; all would kiss his hand and embrace his knees. Every moment brought new masses, which debouched [poured out] in troops from one of the streets, anxious to have their turn. As the Cacciatori [volunteers] gradually cleared the lower part of the town most of the inhabitants came to have a look, and give a greeting to the liberator of Palermo and Sicily."

—Nandor Eber, *The Times,* May 1860

**For Discussion**  How does the reporter, Nandor Eber, view Garibaldi? How might he have written about the campaign for Palermo if he had not had such a view? Might a British reporter have held a more favorable opinion of Garibaldi and the unification of Italy than a reporter from another country? Why or why not?

## ANSWERS

*Possible answers: The reporter has a very favorable view of Garibaldi. If he had had a less favorable view, he might have concentrated on the hardships or loss of life during the campaign instead of on a glowing portrayal of its leader. A British reporter might have held a more favorable opinion of Garibaldi and the unification of Italy than a reporter from a country where the monarchy was not limited by a parliament or other legislative body. Great Britain had become fairly democratic and liberal; a reporter from a more conservative or reactionary country might not have viewed Garibaldi or the unification favorably if he or she thought that revolutionary ideas would threaten security at home.*

Teacher's Guide to Analyzing Movies

## Imperialism in Africa

> 1964; Cy Endfield, Director; Starring Stanley Baker, Michael Caine, Jack Hawkins, Ulla Jacobsson, James Booth, and Ben Nigel Green
>
> 138 minutes, not rated, available on videotape and DVD, color

## WHY WATCH THIS MOVIE?

*Zulu* portrays an episode in the history of British imperialism—the defense of Rorke's Drift, a lonely outpost in South Africa. On January 23, 1879, just 139 British soldiers held off 4,000 Zulu warriors attacking the garrison. The British lost only 15 men; the Zulus counted more than 1,000 dead. For their heroism 11 British men won the Victoria Cross, the empire's highest award for valor.

   *Zulu* was enormously popular in England. It played in some movie theaters for years. Its success can be attributed to its portrayal of the courage and heroism of the British soldiers who refused to abandon Rorke's Drift as the Zulus approached.

   The film includes some historical inaccuracies. The white helmets worn in the film are obvious targets. In reality, British troops dyed their helmets brown with tea. The Zulus did not take their rifles from dead British soldiers; they had purchased them from traders. Despite these flaws, most historians praise the film for its accuracy. At least one scholar has written that the film could serve as a documentary rather than as fiction.

## THE SCENES

**Scene 1** (from 00:03:23 to 00:13:00, 10 minutes) shows the Reverend Witt and his daughter Margareta attending a mass wedding ceremony at the kraal, or compound, of Zulu chieftain Cetshwayo kaMpande (played by a real Zulu chieftain). While acknowledging the greatness of the Zulus, Witt and his daughter are somewhat condescending. Their attitude changes quickly when a messenger interrupts the ceremony. He reveals that Cetshwayo's men have defeated the British forces at Isandhlwana, killing some 1,300 British and colonial troops. Witt and Margareta flee the kraal. *(Note: This scene contains some brief partial nudity among the dancing Zulu women.)*

**Scene 2** (from 00:24:48 to 00:38:18, 14 minutes) starts with the British at Rorke's Drift preparing for battle. When Lieutenant Bromhead disparages the bravery and skill of African troops, Adendorff points out that the Zulus already have defeated the British army once that day. Later, Adendorff explains the Zulu battle tactics, and Lieutenant Chard plans a defense.

**Scene 3** (from 01:56:00 to 02:06:20, 10 minutes) opens with the British having repulsed several Zulu attacks and survived the night, although much of the compound has been destroyed. Chard organizes his men to meet another Zulu assault. Careful organization and mass firepower save the British, and the Zulus again retreat.

## DISCUSSION QUESTIONS BASED ON THE SCENES

1. What do these scenes reveal about European perceptions of Africans? *Possible answer: These episodes reveal the sense of superiority that many Europeans felt during the colonial era.*

2. How did battle tactics of the British and the Zulus differ? What role did technology play in the conflict? *Possible answers: On the offense, the Zulus used the "buffalo strategy," encircling their enemy from the sides. As defenders of the small outpost, the British had few options. They relied heavily on the firepower of their rifles to win the day.*

## WHAT CAN STUDENTS LEARN FROM THESE SCENES?

Students learn how the imperial powers viewed the people who lived in the areas they wanted to colonize. The British and other Europeans often had little respect for native concerns or cultures. The film also vividly illustrates the importance of technology during the heyday of imperialism. As Lieutenant Chard notes at the conclusion of Scene 3, the "miracle" of the British victory results from their superior weapons.

Students will not learn, however, the causes of the Zulu conflict, which are never explained in the motion picture. By the late 1870s the Zulus were a desperate people. Cattle diseases and drought had proven devastating, and the Zulus were fighting for control of pasturage they needed to survive.

## WHAT HAPPENS NEXT? HOW DOES THE STORY END?

The British troops assemble for a roll call. Chard and Bromhead tour the remains of the outpost, and Bromhead declares that he is ashamed by what has happened. Some historians find this statement to be unlikely and out of character for a British officer. In a fictional scene, the Zulus reappear on the hillsides, and the British fear another attack. However, the Zulus have assembled to salute their enemy for their courage—perhaps another unlikely scene. A narrative voice-over lists the soldiers who were later awarded the Victoria Cross.

## IF YOUR CLASS WATCHES THE ENTIRE FILM

Most historians praise *Zulu* for its historical accuracy. However, the film never offers a Zulu perspective of the battle. Although the Zulu warriors are shown to be as brave and courageous as their British counterparts, the film's unwillingness to examine the causes of the conflict makes it a testimony to imperialism rather than an investigation into the historical consequences of colonialism. How might a future director remake *Zulu* so that it offers a more complete historical picture of events in Africa in the 1870s? *Possible answers: Students might answer that the current film portrays the Zulus as a faceless mass without any interesting personalities. Scenes depicting the Zulu warriors as human beings with fears, hopes, and their own visions of the future might improve the film. In addition, some discussion of the causes of the conflict would make the film more historically engaging.*

## GUIDED VIEWING ACTIVITY ANSWERS

1. Margareta finds the ceremony distasteful and offensive.

2. He orders the cook to douse the fire so the Zulus cannot use it to set fire to the thatched roofs.

3. Adendorff uses an image of a buffalo to explain the Zulu attack.

4. The British riflemen form three rows, with one row firing as the other two reload.

5. The British credit their guns, bayonets, and courage.

*Zulu*

# Guided Viewing Activity

## Imperialism in Africa

### SCENE 1

1. What does Margareta Witt think of the Zulu ceremony?

_____

_____

_____

### SCENE 2

2. Why does Lieutenant Chard order the cook to pour the soup on the fire?

_____

_____

_____

3. What animal does Adendorff use to explain the Zulu method of attack?

_____

_____

_____

### SCENE 3

4. How do the British organize their rifleman in order to achieve maximum firepower?

_____

_____

_____

5. What is the source of the "miracle" that has saved the British?

_____

_____

_____

## Analyzing Primary Sources

This fable, as told by Kenyan nationalist Jomo Kenyatta, may enhance your viewing of *Zulu*.

"Once upon a time an elephant made a friendship with a man. One day a heavy thunderstorm broke out, the elephant went to his friend, who had a little hut at the edge of the forest, and said to him: 'My dear good man, will you please let me put my trunk inside your hut to keep it out of this torrential rain?' The man, seeing what situation his friend was in, replied: 'My dear good elephant, my hut is very small, but there is room for your trunk and myself. Please put your trunk in gently.' The elephant thanked his friend, saying: 'You have done me a good deed and one day I shall return your kindness.' But what followed? As soon as the elephant put his trunk inside the hut, slowly he pushed his head inside, and finally flung the man out in the rain, and then lay down comfortably inside his friend's hut, saying: 'My dear good friend, your skin is harder than mine, and as there is not enough room for both of us, you can afford to remain in the rain while I am protecting my delicate skin from the hailstorm.'"

—Jomo Kenyatta, *Facing Mount Kenya,* 1953

**For Discussion** The fable continues with an argument between the man and the elephant, which draws the attention of other jungle animals. The lion, as king of the jungle, appoints a Commission of Enquiry to look into the matter. But the commission is made up of the elephant's friends, including the rhinoceros, buffalo, alligator, fox, and leopard. At the hearing, the elephant testifies that he was protecting his friend's unoccupied hut from a hurricane. The man protests but is quickly silenced. The commission's verdict is that the elephant was protecting the man's interests and was putting the hut to its best economic use. The animals say the dispute arose because of the backwardness of the man's ideas. He is given permission, though, to build a new hut elsewhere. Soon the other animals want it, too. Finally, the man has his revenge on the animals by burning down the hut into which they have all crowded. *Questions:* How does the fable portray Europeans and Africans? How do these portrayals differ from those shown in the film? What insights into the Africans' view of imperialism does this fable provide?

## ANSWERS

*Possible answers: The fable portrays the Europeans as greedy animals and the Africans as an innocent man. The film shows both groups as brave, but the Africans' views of European imperialism are not shown. The fable shows that the Africans viewed imperialism as a takeover of their homes by condescending intruders.*

# Movie Guide

> 1930; Lewis Milestone, Director; Starring Lew Ayres, Louis Wolheim, John Wray, Slim Summerville, Russell Gleason, and Ben Alexander
>
> 133 minutes, not rated, available on videotape and DVD, black and white
>
> This activity applies to the 1930 original of the film. There is also a 1979 remake.

## WHY WATCH THIS MOVIE?

*All Quiet on the Western Front* follows a group of German boys who enlist in the army and experience the tragedies of World War I on the Western Front. Early scenes illustrate the roles that militarism and nationalism played in causing the war. The movie then makes clear, in contrast, how the war's new technologies and tactics horrified the young soldiers. Although the movie focuses on a small band of soldiers, *All Quiet on the Western Front* shows why the Great War shocked the world so deeply.

The film is based on a 1929 novel by German-American writer Erich Maria Remarque. It was an immediate success when it was published. When the Nazis came to power in Germany in the 1930s, however, they ordered the book burned. The Nazis also tried to keep Germans from seeing the film because it showed the dangers of militarism and nationalism. In fact, during the Berlin premiere, Nazis released mice, stink bombs, and sneezing powder into the theater. Although the movie was banned in Germany, it played to packed houses in neighboring countries.

## THE SCENES

**Scene 1** (from 00:04:00 to 00:10:00, 6 minutes) begins with a German schoolteacher encouraging his students to enlist in the army. As he describes the glories of fighting and dying for their country, the young men daydream about what going to war may mean to them. On the teacher's urging, the young men leave as a group to enlist.

**Scene 2** (from 00:31:00 to 00:46:00, 15 minutes) starts at the Western Front in a flimsy bunker. The miseries of life in the trenches are vividly portrayed. One soldier is shot when he panics and runs out to the battlefield. Finally, the signal for combat comes, and the men take up their positions in the trench. French soldiers attack amid heavy artillery fire. After a brutal advance-and-retreat battle that includes vicious hand-to-hand fighting in the trenches, the German soldiers retreat to their original position.

**Scene 3** (from 00:49:00 to 00:53:00, 4 minutes) takes place on a peaceful afternoon. After enjoying a rare hot meal, the soldiers talk about the causes of war and how wars should really be fought.

## DISCUSSION QUESTIONS BASED ON THE SCENES

1. How did the attitudes of the young men change from Scene 1 to Scene 3? What effect did events like those of Scene 2 have on this attitude? *Possible answers: In Scene 1 the young men are excited about enlisting in the army. In Scene 3 their comments show how tired and disillusioned they have become. The horrors of battle as shown in Scene 2 are very different from the glories that the teacher had promised.*

2. Would the movie have been very different if it had been told from the point of view of English or French soldiers, instead of German? Why or why not? *Possible answers: It probably would not have been very different, because trench warfare caused terrible suffering on all sides.*

Teacher's Guide to Analyzing Movies

## WHAT CAN STUDENTS LEARN FROM THESE SCENES?

Students learn that in the early days of the conflict, many people were enthusiastic about the war. The power of nationalism is also clearly shown as the boys are swept up in the teacher's challenge. Then, as they view the war from the soldiers' perspective, students learn about the actual horrors of trench warfare. The scenes also suggest many general questions about war. Scene 3 in particular can lead to discussions about the causes of war, what is gained from war, and the roles of national leaders in wartime.

## WHAT HAPPENS NEXT? HOW DOES THE STORY END?

The war continues. Some of the young men who enlisted together are wounded and die. Paul is hospitalized with a severe wound. When he recovers, he goes home on leave. There he finds that people not involved in the fighting have no idea how terrible it is. Paul visits his old teacher, who, like several other old men, is still talking about the glory of war. In disgust, Paul goes back to the front before his leave is over. He is the only one of the original group still alive. During a lull in the battle, Paul reaches out of a trench to touch a butterfly. The camera shows only his hand as a single gunshot rings out. The hand jerks and then goes limp. In the final scene, a shadowy image of the young men marching off to war plays against a hillside of white crosses.

## IF YOUR CLASS WATCHES THE ENTIRE FILM

Many film historians consider *All Quiet on the Western Front* the first great antiwar film of the sound era. Others have said that it is one of the few old black-and-white films that modern audiences still watch. Do you think the film deserves this reputation? Why or why not? *Possible answers: The film says very little about the political events that led up to World War I. Instead, the focus is on the soldiers' experiences and reactions to battle. Perhaps succeeding generations of viewers feel that those experiences and reactions are common throughout history and the world, no matter which war is being fought. The film's continuing popularity may be due to this timeless quality.*

## GUIDED VIEWING ACTIVITY ANSWERS

1. One boy imagines how proud his father would be if he enlisted. Another sees himself with pretty girls in a big parade.

2. The boys use peer pressure to get the last classmate to join them.

3. Hunger, boredom, constant noise, constant danger, lack of sleep, rats, and panic make life in the bunker hard for the soldiers.

4. The battlefield has no plants, is pitted with holes, and has barbed wire strung across it.

5. They do not hate the enemy soldiers.

### *All Quiet on the Western Front*  Guided Viewing Activity

**SCENE 1**

1. What do some of the boys daydream about while the teacher is urging them to enlist?

_____

_____

_____

2. At first, not all the boys want to volunteer. What happens to change that situation?

_____

_____

_____

**SCENE 2**

3. What are some of the things that make life in the bunker so bad?

_____

_____

_____

4. What does the battlefield look like?

_____

_____

_____

**SCENE 3**

5. How do the men feel about the enemy soldiers that they face on the battlefield?

_____

_____

_____

## Analyzing Primary Sources

These eyewitness battlefield accounts by soldiers on both sides of World War I may enhance your viewing of *All Quiet on the Western Front.*

**Source 1: From an English soldier in the trenches at Gallipoli, 1915**

"We set to work to bury people. We pushed them into the sides of the trench but bits of them kept getting uncovered and sticking out, like people in a badly made bed. Hands were the worst; they would escape from the sand, pointing, begging—even waving! There was one which we all shook when we passed, saying, 'Good morning', in a posh voice. Everybody did it . . . The flies entered the trenches at night and lined them completely with a density which was like moving cloth. We killed millions by slapping our spades along the trench walls . . . We wept, not because we were frightened but because we were so dirty."

—Leonard Thompson, from *Akenfield,* by Ronald Blythe

**For Discussion**  How does Thompson's description of life in the trenches compare to what is shown in *All Quiet on the Western Front*?

**Source 2: From an Austrian soldier on the Eastern Front, 1915**

"Charge! Now the great day had come, the day for which I too had been longing . . . I wanted to settle this thing on my own and to look the enemy straight in the face. A hero's death—fair enough! But I had no wish to be trampled to death like a worm. The Russians had lured us into a trap . . . I felt a dull blow on my temple.

The sun and the moon were both shining at once and my head ached like mad. What on earth was I to do with this scent of flowers? Some flower—I couldn't remember its name however I racked my brains. And all that yelling round me. . . I tried to say something, but my mouth was stiff with blood, which was beginning to congeal."

—Oskar Kokoschka, from *My Life, transla*ted by David Britt, 1974

**For Discussion**  How is Kokoschka's attitude at the beginning of the passage reflected in the film?

## ANSWERS

**Source 1** *Possible answer: Although burial within the trenches is not shown in the film, the contrast between the horrors of the trenches and the humor the soldiers display is similar.*

**Source 2** *Possible answer: Kokoschka's attitude is similar to the young soldiers' enthusiasm for the war as shown in the film.*

## The Russian Revolution

---

1965; David Lean, Director; Starring Omar Sharif, Julie Christie, Geraldine Chaplin, Rod Steiger, Alec Guinness, and Tom Courtenay

197 minutes, not rated, available on videotape and DVD, color

This activity applies to the 1965 original of the film. There are also 2002 and 2006 remakes.

---

## WHY WATCH THIS MOVIE?

*Doctor Zhivago* is a love story set against the historical backdrop of the Russian Revolution. Yuri Zhivago is a doctor and a poet who has little interest in politics. However, his life is profoundly altered by Russia's entry into World War I and the Bolshevik Revolution. He is forced to fight with the Bolsheviks, or Reds, in their civil war against the Whites, who opposed Bolshevik rule.

The movie is based on Boris Pasternak's 1957 novel of the same name. Soviet officials banned the novel because it did not present the revolution in a favorable light. Director David Lean saw *Doctor Zhivago* as a vehicle for an epic love story. The film won five Academy Awards, including Best Costume Design and Best Cinematography. However, it was not a critical success. Many reviewers noted that the lead character, Zhivago, is a passive figure with whom audiences had difficulty identifying. The plot moves rather slowly. Those critics who enjoyed the movie pointed to its grand sweep, including the lovely vistas of forests and mountains, although the movie was not filmed in the Soviet Union. The beautiful landscapes were in Spain, Finland, and Canada.

## THE SCENES

**Scene 1** (from 01:12:37 to 01:21:18, 9 minutes) opens with enthusiastic crowds hailing the volunteers who are marching off to fight in World War I. In a narrative voice-over, Yevgraf Zhivago, the doctor's half brother, describes the Russian experiences in the war. When deserting troops encounter replacement soldiers on a road, violence breaks out. The scene ends with Lara and Zhivago aiding wounded soldiers.

**Scene 2** (from 00:31:00 to 00:46:00, 15 minutes) shows Tonya welcoming Zhivago home at war's end. The family suffers hardships, as food and fuel are in short supply. Party officials threaten and bully everyone. Yevgraf, now a Bolshevik official, warns Zhivago that party leaders are unhappy with his poetry. The doctor and his family flee Moscow. During the wretched train ride eastward, they witness firsthand the devastation of the civil war between the Reds and the Whites.

## DISCUSSION QUESTIONS BASED ON THE SCENES

1. Why are the Russian troops willing to abandon the trenches and disobey their officers? *Possible answer: The Eastern Front was a place of terror and misery for the soldiers. They fought without adequate supplies. After they desert, they reject arguments that they have a duty to Russia, which they believed had abandoned them on the front lines.*

2. How has the revolution changed the lives of the Russian people? *Possible answer: The revolution has brought food and fuel shortages. Government officials threaten people who do not cooperate. Wealthy families such as the Zhivagos have lost their property, but the poor people suffer even more, as is shown in the burning village that the passengers see from the train.*

## WHAT CAN STUDENTS LEARN FROM THESE SCENES?

These scenes provide insight into the enormous suffering that Russians endured in the 1910s and 1920s. World War I took the lives of about 2 million soldiers, with another 6 million wounded or captured. The people in the cities labored in the factories only to discover that bread was so scarce it had to be rationed. The Bolshevik Revolution brought only more misery. The nation was racked by civil war, and the communists used terror to control the civilian population. *Doctor Zhivago* also illustrates the fear that Russians felt when they had to deal with communist party officials. On a broader scope, students can see how events can affect political thought.

## WHAT HAPPENS NEXT? HOW DOES THE STORY END?

Zhivago learns that the dreaded Bolshevik Strelnikov is the husband of his great love, Lara. The doctor is forced to serve in the Red Army during the civil war; meanwhile, his family escapes to Paris. Zhivago deserts the army and is reunited with Lara. He learns that the Bolsheviks will kill him if they find him. Zhivago sends Lara away, promising to join her later. He never does. Eight years later he believes he sees her as he is riding a Moscow streetcar. He runs after a blonde woman in the street but suffers a heart attack and dies. Lara attends his funeral. Yefgrav explains that Lara later vanished and probably died in a labor camp.

## IF YOUR CLASS WATCHES THE ENTIRE FILM

*Doctor Zhivago* focuses on the experiences of one man during a period of turmoil and terror in Russian history. However, the film does not explain the causes of the Russian Revolution that led to those experiences. What scenes might you include to provide greater historical understanding of this era in Russian life? *Possible answers: Student answers will vary. Some students might include scenes of the czar or of Lenin arguing in favor of revolution. Other students might show scenes of suffering that would lead the Russian people to support the overthrow of their government.*

## GUIDED VIEWING ACTIVITY ANSWERS

1. The Bolsheviks hope that the war will end with a Russian defeat that will spark a workers' revolt against the czarist government.

2. After the officer falls into a barrel, a deserting soldier shoots him.

3. Zhivago concludes that the old man is starving to death.

4. He obtains the firewood by stealing it, ripping the slats from a fence.

5. Yevgraf Zhivago tells his half brother to leave Moscow immediately.

**Doctor Zhivago**

# Guided Viewing Activity
## The Russian Revolution

## SCENE 1

1. What do the Bolsheviks hope will happen as the Russian troops fight in World War I?

_____

_____

_____

2. What happens to the officer who warns the deserting troops that the Germans are near?

_____

_____

_____

## SCENE 2

3. What is killing the elderly man whom Zhivago examines?

_____

_____

_____

4. How does Zhivago obtain firewood?

_____

_____

_____

5. What advice does Zhivago receive from his half brother?

_____

_____

_____

## Analyzing Primary Sources

These primary sources may enhance your viewing of *Dr. Zhivago*.

**Source 1: From a treatise by V. I. Lenin**

"Therefore any belittlement of socialist ideology, any dismissal of it signifies the strengthening of bourgeois ideology. There is discussion of spontaneity. But spontaneous development of the workers movement leads to its subordination to the bourgeois ideology."

—V. I. Lenin, *What Is To Be Done?*, 1902

**For Discussion** What does Lenin say will happen if anyone criticizes socialism? How does his view compare to personal freedoms listed in the U.S. Bill of Rights?

**Source 2: From a member of an international relief effort sent to Russia in 1921**

"There were forty homes here for abandoned or wandering children. I went into a number of them and they were all alike in general character. In big, bare rooms the children were naked and huddled together like little monkeys for warmth. There was no other warmth as there was no fuel. Their clothes had been burnt because of the lice which spread typhus among them. There were no other clothes to replace their ragged old sheepskins and woollen garments. Often it was too late to check the epidemic of typhus and thousands died and now were dying."

—Philip Gibbs, "Famine in Russia," 1921

**For Discussion** In Scene 2 of the film, you saw what the Zhivago family witnesses from the train. What details does Gibbs's account provide about the famine in the Russian countryside? How does his account contrast with Lenin's statement?

### ANSWERS

**Source 1** *Possible answers: He says that any criticism of socialism strengthens its opponent, "bourgeois ideology." His view conflicts with the freedom of speech guaranteed in the U.S. Bill of Rights.*

**Source 2** *Possible answers: Gibbs's account gives graphic details about how the Russian children were affected by the famine. Some students may note that Lenin's praise of socialism seems naïve or unrealistic in comparison, considering the human disaster that resulted partly from the application of its principles. Other students may hold other opinions.*

Teacher's Guide to Analyzing Movies

1987; Jack Gold, Director; Starring Rutger Hauer, Alan Arkin, Joanna Pacula, Harmut Becker, Jack Shepherd, Emil Wolk, and Simon Gregor

120 minutes, not rated, available on videotape and DVD, color

## WHY WATCH THIS MOVIE?

*Escape from Sobibor* chronicles events in 1943 at Sobibor, a Nazi death camp in eastern Poland. As many as 250,000 Jews were murdered at Sobibor. About 600 Jewish workers were kept alive to serve the Nazis and maintain the camp. The Jewish prisoners realized that they were doomed unless they acted, so they staged a mass escape in October, 1943. About 300 inmates made it outside the camp gates, but most were soon killed. Only 50 to 60 managed to survive the war.

    *Escape from Sobibor* was produced for broadcast television. Director Jack Gold was initially reluctant to work on a film about the Holocaust. He believed that dramatic portrayals could never capture the horrors of that event. However, Gold changed his mind, in part because he believed that the Sobibor escape deserved to be more widely known.

    To ensure that the film was as faithful to history as possible, survivors of the Sobibor escape served as consultants, approving each line of dialogue and every scene. As a result, *Escape from Sobibor* has received positive reviews from critics. It manages to convey the horrors of the Holocaust and the heroism of its victims without engaging in extremely graphic portrayals of violence. The film does contain some scenes of beatings and shootings, however. In addition, it includes a brief scene in which naked inmates are herded into "showers" for extermination.

## THE SCENES

**Scene 1** (from 00:03:39 to 00:18:00, 15 minutes) begins with Jewish workers in line, awaiting a trainload of new arrivals to Sobibor. In the distance they hear gunshots, which they know means that an escape attempt has failed. German officers oversee the offloading of Jewish refugees, who are misled into believing they have arrived at a work camp. Individuals with useful skills are removed from the main group. Most of the Jews then head for the camp under the belief that they will be disinfected in showers. The camp workers know, however, that these new arrivals are being led to their deaths. Nazi brutality quickly becomes apparent when a German shoots an old man for striking an officer.

**Scene 2** (from 00:48:48 to 00:54:35, 6 minutes) takes place after an escape attempt. Two men managed to run away from a work detail, but another 13 have been captured. The Germans force the camp workers to witness the execution of the 13. To drive home the lesson that escape attempts will not be tolerated, the Nazis force the condemned men to select an additional 13 people to die with them.

## DISCUSSION QUESTIONS BASED ON THE SCENES

  1. Why do the new arrivals cooperate with the Nazis? How do the Nazis try to put them at ease? Why do the Jewish workers who know the truth about the camp remain silent? *Possible answers: The new arrivals are exhausted and confused and have no idea that the Germans are operating a death camp. The Germans play pleasant music and tell numerous lies about the camp. The workers remain silent because to reveal the truth would save no lives and result in their own deaths.*

Teacher's Guide to Analyzing Movies

2. What difficulties do the prisoners face in planning an escape? *Possible answer: Students might note that the Germans are highly trained, organized, and heavily armed. The prisoners have no weapons and are ordinary people who lack the skills necessary to overwhelm the guards or plan an elaborate escape. The prisoners also know that a failed attempt will lead to the death of innocent comrades.*

## WHAT CAN STUDENTS LEARN FROM THESE SCENES?

Students learn that the Germans used deception and brutality to control the prisoners whom they killed at the death camps. The first scene reveals that cooperation with the Germans was based on fear, confusion, and ignorance of the purpose of the camps. It also explains why some Jews were willing to cooperate with the Nazis. The second scene shows the difficulties that camp inmates faced in resisting the Nazis, explaining why prisoner revolts were very rare. (There were only three large revolts, and Sobibor was the only camp from which there was a mass escape.)

## WHAT HAPPENS NEXT? HOW DOES THE STORY END?

The Jewish prisoners' leaders realize that the escape they have been planning will lead to the death of innocent people in the camp. They decide that any escape must be a mass effort, with every prisoner given the opportunity to flee. The arrival of a group of Russian Jews who are also soldiers provides the inmates with the direction and skill they need to plan an effective escape. On one afternoon they quickly murder several German officers and rush the gates. Most of the prisoners are killed by machine gun fire or by mines that ring the camp. A narrative voice-over at the film's conclusion discusses the fate of the various major characters in the film.

## IF YOUR CLASS WATCHES THE ENTIRE FILM

Creating dramatic portrayals of horrific events such as the Holocaust is problematic. Film historians debate the wisdom of making such motion pictures and question their accuracy and authenticity. Do you think that the Holocaust is a subject appropriate for a motion picture? Do you think that making a film about a rare event such as the escape at the Sobibor camp offers viewers an accurate understanding of the Holocaust? *Possible answers: Some students will state that films cannot offer viewers a complete understanding of the Holocaust and might argue that documentaries are more appropriate. Others may argue that movies introduce viewers to important historical events about which they might otherwise remain ignorant. Concerning the Sobibor film, some will note that the escape was so unusual that it might lead some viewers to think that prisoners who did not revolt were cowardly. Others may argue that the film showed how difficult resistance in the camps was and reveals the bravery with which the victims of the Holocaust met their fates.*

## GUIDED VIEWING ACTIVITY ANSWERS

1. They cry out for water.

2. They seek shoemakers, tailors, and seamstresses.

3. He does not want to kill the old man in front of the prisoners because that might cause them to panic.

4. The executions are punishment for an escape attempt.

5. Anyone who does not watch the execution will be killed.

**_Escape From Sobibor_**  ## Guided Viewing Activity
### The Holocaust

## SCENE 1

1. What do the people cry out for as they arrive at the train station?

_____

_____

_____

2. What kinds of workers do the Nazis seek?

_____

_____

_____

3. Why does the German officer wait before killing the old man?

_____

_____

_____

## SCENE 2

4. Why are the Germans executing some of the camp workers?

_____

_____

_____

5. How do the Nazis force the other prisoners to watch the execution?

_____

_____

_____

## Analyzing Primary Sources

In this excerpt a Sobibor survivor interviews a Nazi who had executed the survivor's family at the prison camp. The passage may enhance your viewing of *Escape from Sobibor*.

**From an interview conducted by Thomas T. Blatt of Karl Frenzel**

"I had many questions to ask Frenzel. As a survivor I had often wondered what a Nazi thought of the film 'Holocaust'. Had he seen it? He shook his head. Did he think any film or documentary could show it the way it was? 'No,' he said, 'the reality was much worse . . . it was so terrible that it can not be described.'

"Suddenly, though I tried to block it out, a scene flashed across my mind: my friend, Leon, being beaten to death, slowly and the horror of being forced to watch his agony. Another scene flashed . . . Standing, listening to the muffled screams from the gas chambers . . . and knowing that men, women and children were dying in horrible pain, naked, as I worked sorting their clothing . . .

"He continued, '. . . I can understand that you can never forget, but I can't either. I've dreamed about it all of the sixteen years I spent in prison. Just as you dream about it, I dream about it too.' Surely he wasn't comparing his nightmares to mine . . . or was he saying his conscience was bothering him?

"I had another leading question. What had happened to the Dutch Jews? He immediately knew what I meant. Like a superior officer, he answered swiftly and to the point, 'A Polish Kapo told me some Dutch Jews were organizing an escape, so I relayed it to Deputy Commandant Niemann and he ordered the seventy-two Jews to be executed.' He failed to mention that he alone led them to be killed. And I could not help noting that his voice and bearing were more forceful now and there was a feeling of competence and pride about his work . . ."

—Thomas T. Blatt, "The Confrontation with a Murderer," 1984

**For Discussion** How does Blatt seem to interpret Frenzel's attitude about what he did at Sobibor? Do students agree with Frenzel's statement that films cannot capture the horrors of the Holocaust? Why or why not?

### ANSWERS

*Possible answers: Blatt seems to feel that Frenzel is still defending his actions to some extent. Most students will probably agree that no film could portray the horrors of the Holocaust.*

## Indian Independence

1984; Christopher Morahan and Jim O'Brien, Directors; Starring Peggy Ashcroft, Derrick Branche, Charles Dance, Geraldine James, Rachel Kempson, and Art Malik

750 minutes, not rated, available on videotape and DVD, color

## WHY WATCH THIS MOVIE?

*The Jewel in the Crown* is set during the last days of British rule in India. The program follows several characters, British and Indian, in the years 1942 to 1947. The historical backdrop is World War II and the struggle for Indian independence, but the mini-series focuses on the corrosive effects of imperialism on the personal lives of the people in the British Raj.

The first featured story is the tragic romance that develops between Daphne Manners, a young Englishwoman, and Hari Kumer. Hari is an Indian who was raised in England and attended an elite school there. Recently returned to India, he sees himself as English rather than Indian—he does not even speak Hindi. The English, however, do not accept Hari as one of their own. Ronald Merrick, a British police officer, hates Hari because Daphne has fallen in love with the handsome young Indian. Their complicated relationship, which ends with Daphne dead and Hari wrongfully imprisoned, represents the injustices of imperial rule.

*The Jewel in the Crown* was remarkably popular when it aired in England in 1984, attracting some 8 million viewers. Historians have noted that in the early 1980s a number of films about the era of British imperialism attracted large audiences. The 1980s were a period of economic and social turmoil in the United Kingdom, and these programs might have represented nostalgia for Britain's lost glory. If that is so, *The Jewel in the Crown* was perhaps a troubling reminder of the flaws of the British Empire.

## THE SCENES

**Scene 1** (from 00:58:38 to 01:10:, 12 minutes) opens with Ronald Merrick bringing home Daphne Manners after an unsuccessful first date. Merrick expresses his anger toward Mohandas Gandhi. The following day the monsoon rains arrive. Daphne and Hari meet at the sanctuary, where the poor receive medical care. Later, they meet again and go bicycling. As they sit in the Bibighar Gardens, Hari makes a frank confession to Daphne, telling her that he hates India.

**Scene 2** (from 01:27:08 to 01:32:50, 5 minutes) is a conversation between Hari and Sister Ludmilla at the sanctuary. Hari discusses the events that led up to his arrest several weeks earlier. He explains that he had seen an old English schoolmate that day. However, his friend did not even recognize him, as now Hari is just another nameless Indian. Hari's Indian friends mock his pretensions and together they burn his hat, symbolizing a rejection of things British. Hari concludes his story with an account of his arrest and questioning by Merrick.

## DISCUSSION QUESTIONS BASED ON THE SCENES

1. How do the English perceive the Indians that they rule? *Possible answer: Students might contrast the behavior of Ronald Merrick and another Englishman, Colin, with that of Daphne Manners and Sister Ludmilla. Colin does not see the Indians at all, while Merrick dislikes them to the point of hatred. Daphne is intrigued by India and is clearly attracted to Hari. Sister Ludmilla has given her life to helping the poor of India.*

2. What are Hari's attitudes toward the British and toward himself as an Indian who perceives himself as British? *Possible answer: Students should note that Hari is very conflicted. He admires the English as his reminiscence of his school days reveals. Their treatment of him in India has led Hari to hate himself rather than to feel contempt for the Raj.*

## WHAT CAN STUDENTS LEARN FROM THESE SCENES?

Students learn about the abuses that resulted from imperial rule. With the exception of Daphne Manners, the British are contemptuous of the Indians. The character of Hari Kumer serves as a case study of individuals caught between two cultures who feel they belong to neither. Students can also gain insight into details of daily life at the time. *The Jewel in the Crown* was filmed in India, and the producers paid close attention to the simplest details, down to the length of the khaki shorts that British soldiers wore. Finally, the scene in the sanctuary offers a glimpse of the tremendous poverty that still burdens India today.

## WHAT HAPPENS NEXT? HOW DOES THE STORY END?

Daphne and Hari fall in love. After Daphne is brutally assaulted at the Bibighar Gardens, Merrick accuses Hari of the crime. Hari is innocent but does not defend himself in order to keep his word to Daphne, who wants their romance kept secret. Merrick tortures Hari, who is then imprisoned for a crime he did not commit. Daphne dies in childbirth. The remainder of the series focuses on the experiences of other English families in India as the nation moves toward independence and partition. Merrick is the one recurring character. He remains a sadistic and troubled man, and meets with a violent end.

## IF YOUR CLASS WATCHES THE ENTIRE FILM

The Jewel in the Crown won critical praise and set new standards for television broadcasting in the 1980s. Some critics argued, however, that it did not provide a balanced view of life in the Raj, as with few exceptions the main characters are British rather than Indian. Do you think that the series would be improved by the inclusion of additional Indian characters whose stories are told in detail? *Possible answer: Some students may argue that the focus of the series is British imperialism, and that it is fitting that the program focuses on the British in India. Others may argue that the Raj affected the Indian people at least as much as it did the British, and that the series lacks balance without additional attention paid to its major Indian characters.*

## GUIDED VIEWING ACTIVITY ANSWERS

1. Merrick fears that Gandhi's actions will lead to trouble.

2. Daphne goes outside and lets the refreshing rain fall on her.

3. Hari hates the beggars, the crowds, the heat, the bugs, and himself for not being Indian and English at the same time.

4. Hari is devastated when Colin does not even notice him.

5. Hari's friends burn his hat.

*The Jewel in the Crown*  Guided Viewing Activity

### Indian Independence

## SCENE 1

1. Why does Merrick want Daphne to use his car?

_____

_____

_____

2. How does Daphne react to the arrival of the monsoon rains?

_____

_____

_____

3. What does Hari hate about India?

_____

_____

_____

## SCENE 2

4. What happens when Hari sees Colin at the cricket match?

_____

_____

_____

5. How do Hari's friends celebrate his rejection of his English past?

_____

_____

_____

## Analyzing Primary Sources

These comments by two prominent Indian leaders may enhance your
viewing of *The Jewel in the Crown*:

**Source 1: From an Indian intellectual, educator, and politician**

> "To sum up the whole, the British rule has been: morally, a great blessing;
> politically, peace and order on one hand, blunders on the other; materially,
> impoverishment, relieved as far as the railway and other loans go. The
> natives call the British system 'Sakar ki Churi,' the knife of sugar. That is
> to say, there is no oppression, it is all smooth and sweet, but it is the knife,
> notwithstanding . . . Our great misfortune is that you do not know our
> wants. When you will know our real wishes, I have not the least doubt that
> you would do justice. The genius and spirit of the British people is fair play
> and justice."
>
> —Dadabhai Naoroji, *The Benefits of British Rule,* 1871

**For Discussion**  How does Naoroji's summary of British rule compare to
how British rule is shown in *The Jewel in the Crown*?

**Source 2: From Mohandas K. Gandhi**

> "It is not we who have to do as you [the English] wish, but it is you who
> have to do as we wish. You may keep the riches that you have drained
> away from this land, but you may not drain riches henceforth. Your
> function will be, if you so wish, to police India; you must abandon the idea
> of deriving any commercial benefit from us. We hold the civilization that
> you support to be the reverse of civilization. We consider our civilization
> to be far superior to yours . . . We have hitherto said nothing because we
> have been cowed down, but you need not consider that you have not hurt
> our feelings by your conduct."
>
> —Mohandas K. Gandhi, *Indian Home Rule,* 1909

**For Discussion**  India gained its independence 38 years after Gandhi wrote
this essay, in 1947. Had the English treatment of India become more
sensitive to Indian feelings by that time? On what do you base your answer?

## ANSWERS

**Source 1** *Possible answer: The film's depiction is less favorable, but the more positive parts of
Naoroji's summary reflect some of Hari's feelings for the country where he was raised.*

**Source 2** *Possible answers: Students may note that, at least as depicted in the film, the English
treatment of India had not become more sensitive.*

2000; Roger Donaldson, Director; Starring Kevin Costner, Bruce Greenwood, Steven Culp, Dylan Baker, Bill Smitrovich, and Henry Strozier

145 minutes, rated PG-13, available on videotape and DVD, color

## WHY WATCH THIS MOVIE?

*Thirteen Days* chronicles the Cuban missile crisis of October, 1962. That month U-2 surveillance flights revealed that the Soviet Union was constructing nuclear missile sites in Cuba. This information raised the specter of a successful first strike against cities in the United States. President John F. Kennedy quickly convened his top advisers in a group known as the Executive Committee, or EXCOMM. The film shows the pressures that built up on Kennedy as he avoided a nuclear war with the Soviet Union.

## THE SCENES

**Scene 1** (from 00:13:20 to 00:23:37, 10 minutes) opens with a meeting between President Kennedy and members of his top advisers. Everyone present agrees that the missiles cannot remain in Cuba. After the meeting, the president, his brother Attorney General Robert Kennedy, and political adviser Kenneth O'Donnell agree to form EXCOMM. At the EXCOMM meeting later that night, former secretary of state Dean Acheson offers a gloomy prediction of the events that will take place if the United States attacks the missile sites. Kennedy leaves the meeting without announcing a decision.

**Scene 2** (from 01:06:51 to 01:13:28, 7 minutes) begins as Kennedy has decided to establish a naval quarantine around Cuba. (Under international law, declaring a blockade could have been considered an act of war, so Kennedy used the term *quarantine* to describe the U.S. action.) In a private conversation before the quarantine takes effect, he compares the situation to the events that led to World War I. Kenneth O'Donnell then heads home in a sequence that shows the public's anxiety about the crisis. The next morning the quarantine goes into effect. At first it appears as if the Soviets will violate the quarantine, but the Soviet ships slow and then stop before reaching the quarantine line.

## DISCUSSION QUESTIONS BASED ON THE SCENES

1. What options do Kennedy's advisers present to him? If you had been an adviser, what would you have recommended under these circumstances? *Possible answers: All the options presented to Kennedy involve military action, as the possibility of a political resolution is dismissed. Some students might favor military action, while others will note that the possibility of a nuclear war makes it essential to find a diplomatic solution to the crisis.*

2. What risks were involved in establishing the quarantine? What might have happened had the U.S. Navy fired on the Soviet submarine? *Possible answers: The quarantine raised the possibility of U.S. ships firing on Soviet vessels, which could have led to a wider war. Had the United States attacked the Soviet ship, the Soviets might have regarded the incident as an act of war.*

## WHAT CAN STUDENTS LEARN FROM THESE SCENES?

Students learn how close the United States and the Soviet Union came to a nuclear war during the Cuban missile crisis. The scenes also reveal the important role of the U.S. president in making major foreign policy decisions; one person's personality and actions affect everyone. Kennedy was under considerable pressure from many of his top advisers to attack Cuba. He resisted the desire to turn to military force to remedy the crisis, instead choosing a course that led to a resolution that cost only one American life, that of a U-2 pilot shot down on a surveillance flight.

## WHAT HAPPENS NEXT? HOW DOES THE STORY END?

The quarantine did not end the crisis. U.S. ambassador Adlai Stevenson confronts Soviet officials at the United Nations. The possibility of a nuclear exchange remains real as one Soviet ship crosses the quarantine line. As tensions rise, a Soviet agent approaches an ABC newsman with an offer from Soviet leader Nikita Khrushchev. If the United States pledges not to invade Cuba, the Soviet Union will dismantle its nuclear sites in Cuba. The deal falls through, and the shooting down of a U-2 plane over Cuba makes war appear likely. Kennedy argues that diplomacy still has a chance. Acting on a letter from Khrushchev, Kennedy argues that a deal to dismantle U.S. missiles in Turkey for the Soviet missiles in Cuba might work. The deal is made, and the Cuban missile crisis comes to an end.

## IF YOUR CLASS WATCHES THE ENTIRE FILM

Historians admired *Thirteen Days* for its accurate depiction of the Cuban missile crisis. However, some were troubled by the portrayal of American military leaders, such as of Curtis LeMay. Do any scenes in *Thirteen Days* seem to be biased in their portrayal of military officials? If so, why? Or does the audience have enough information on which to base an opinion about the portrayals' fairness? *Possible answers: Students might point to the contempt that officers such as Curtis LeMay express toward President Kennedy as a biased portrayal. Students may also note that they need more information on the historical LeMay before forming an opinion about whether or not his portrayal is biased.*

## GUIDED VIEWING ACTIVITY ANSWERS

1.  Kennedy's advisers claim that the United States will have only five minutes warning.

2. They recommend an attack on the missile sites followed by an invasion of Cuba.

3. He predicts a Soviet attack on Berlin, which might result in a nuclear war.

4. Anxiety shows in the faces of the men waiting for newspapers and in the long line of people waiting to enter the church.

5. The Soviet ships do not cross the quarantine line.

# Guided Viewing Activity

## The Cold War

### SCENE 1

1. How much warning time would the United States have if the Soviets launched missiles from Cuba?

_____

_____

_____

2. What do the officers from the Joints Chiefs of Staff recommend at the EXCOMM meeting?

_____

_____

_____

3. What does Dean Acheson predict will happen after an attack on the missile sites?

_____

_____

_____

### SCENE 2

4. How does this scene illustrate the public anxiety over the Cuban missile crisis?

_____

_____

_____

### SCENE 3

5. How do the Soviets respond to the quarantine?

_____

_____

_____

## Analyzing Primary Sources

These excerpts from speeches made before the United Nations Security Council may enhance your viewing of *Thirteen Days*:

**Source 1: From the U.S. representative to the United Nations, Adlai Stevenson**

"Last night, the President of the United States reported the recent alarming military developments in Cuba . . . In view of this transformation of Cuba into a base for offensive weapons of sudden mass destruction, the President announced the initiation of a strict quarantine on all offensive military weapons under shipment to Cuba. He did so because, in the view of my Government, the recent developments in Cuba—the importation of the cold war into the heart of the Americas—constitute a threat to the peace of this hemisphere, and, indeed, to the peace of the world."

—Adlai Stevenson, October 23, 1962

**For Discussion**  What terms and phrases did Stevenson use to convince his audience of the situation's seriousness?

**Source 2: From the Soviet representative to the United Nations, V. A. Zorin**

"The peoples of the world must clearly realize, however, that in openly embarking on this venture the United States of America is taking a step along the road which leads to a thermo-nuclear world war. Such is the heavy price which the world may have to pay for the present reckless and irresponsible actions of the United States . . . No State, no matter how powerful it may be, has any right to rule on the quantities or types of arms which another State considers necessary for its defence. According to the United Nations Charter, each State has the right to defend itself and to possess weapons to ensure its security."

—V. A. Zorin, October 23, 1962

**For Discussion**  How does Zorin's characterization of the weapons and the general threat compare to Stevenson's?

## ANSWERS

**Source 1**  *Possible answers: He used some emotionally powerful phrases, including sudden mass destruction, offensive, the heart of the Americas, threat to the peace, and so on.*

**Source 2**  *Possible answer: Zorin said the weapons were for defense, while Stevenson characterized them as offensive. Both representatives said that the other country's actions threatened world peace.*

Teacher's Guide to Analyzing Movies